A
Child
Interviewer's
Guidebook

Interpersonal Violence:
The Practice Series

Jon R. Conte, Series Editor

In this series...

A
Child
Interviewer's
Guidebook

Wendy Bourg
Raymond Broderick
Robin Flagor
Donna Meeks Kelly
Diane Lang Ervin
Judy Butler

Interpersonal Violence:
The Practice Series

SAGE Publications
International Educational and Professional Publisher
Thousand Oaks   London   New Delhi

For information:

SAGE Publications, Inc.
2455 Teller Road
Thousand Oaks, California 91320
E-mail: order@sagepub.com

SAGE Publications Ltd.
6 Bonhill Street
London EC2A 4PU
United Kingdom

SAGE Publications India Pvt. Ltd.
M-32 Market
Greater Kailash I
New Delhi 110 048 India

Printed in the United States of America

Library of Congress Cataloging-in-Publication Data

A child interviewer's guidebook / by Wendy Bourg . . . [et al.].
    p. cm. — (Interpersonal violence; v. 23)
    Includes bibliographical references and index.
    ISBN 0-7619-1762-4 (cloth: alk. paper)
    ISBN 0-7619-1763-2 (pbk.: alk. paper)
    1. Child abuse—Investigation. 2. Interviewing in child abuse. I.
Bourg, Wendy. II. Series.
    HV8079.C46 C565 1999
    363.2'595554—dc21   98-40282

This book is printed on acid-free paper.

99 00 01 02 03 04 05 7 6 5 4 3 2 1

Acquisition Editor:	C. Terry Hendrix
Editorial Assistant:	Mary Ann Vail
Production Editor:	Denise Santoyo
Editorial Assistant:	Nevair Kabakian
Typesetter/Designer:	Christina M. Hill
Indexer:	Teri Greenberg

Contents

Introduction

The Child Interviewer's Guidebook was originally developed and published in Oregon, at the request of the Health Advisory Council on Child Abuse, a group convened by the Oregon legislature to ensure that child abuse evaluators in Oregon are highly skilled and well-trained The Health Advisory Council requested that guidelines be written to provide interviewers with a clear, accessible summary of accumulated knowledge in the field of child interviewing.

The guidebook was written by a committee, which included the following members:

Wendy Bourg, Ph.D., Chairperson, C. A. R. E. S. N.W. Program, Portland, OR
Robin Flagor, B.S.W., Member, C. A. R. E. S. Program, Klamath Falls, OR
Raymond Broderick, B.A., Member, Child Advocacy Center, Eugene, OR
Donna Meeks Kelly, J.D., Legal Consultant, Wasco County, OR

The guidebook was written collaboratively. Before many of the chapters were written, the group brainstormed ideas for content. Each chapter was then written by a primary author, critiqued by the group, and edited by Dr. Bourg. Diane Lang Ervin, LCSW, of the KIDS Center in Bend, sat on the committee for 14 months and authored the first draft of the chapter on videotaping. Judy Butler, MEd, of C. A. R. E. S. NW in Portland, guest-authored the chapter on working with special needs children. As with the other chapters, the committee critiqued and Dr. Bourg edited these two chapters.

Once a draft of the guidebook was created, many individuals and groups provided feedback. We are very grateful for the comments of several national experts, including Kathleen Faller, PhD; Amye Warren, PhD; Anne Walker, PhD; Barbara Boat, PhD; and Marcia Morgan, PhD The comments of these experts contributed invaluable insights and functioned as a check that the guidebook was consistent with national views of appropriate practice.

In Oregon, the guidebook was widely reviewed. We would like to thank the Center Network group (directors for all child abuse assessment and advocacy centers in Oregon), the Oregon District Attorney's Association, and the following individuals for the many suggestions they provided to improve this book: Emmy Sloan, MEd; Janvier Slick, MSW, MA, CAMI Coordinator for the State Office of Services to Children and Families; Judith Hylton, MS; Susan Reichert, MD; and Karen Tracy, JD.

We would like to extend a special thank you to Judy Butler for her 10 years of dedication to child interviewing in Oregon. Along with most other child interviewers in Oregon, we have each benefited from her expert consultation and her warm support.

Finally, the creation of this guidebook was a volunteer effort. Every committee activity took time away from our jobs and our families. We are grateful to our families and to Emmy Sloan, Michelle Munsie, and Bernard Smith for helping us find the time to make this project possible.

❏ **Statement of Purpose**

The primary purpose of these guidelines is to promote consistency in the quality of care provided to children when they are evaluated for possible abuse. The authors feel strongly that the best method for improving child interviewing is to ensure that interviewers receive training in integrating research and clinical practice. These guidelines were written as part of a training package designed to provide child abuse evaluators with essential educational resources.

These guidelines are intended for use among professionals working in child abuse assessment centers. Although they may be useful in other settings (e.g., brief initial interviews by child protection workers or law enforcement officers), some of the principles stated herein will apply exclusively to center-based assessments.

The recommendations contained in this document are tailored to child evaluations that concentrate on (a) eliciting reliable statements about possible abuse and (b) maximizing the amount of information gained from the child, given the child's age, circumstances, and readiness to talk. Although the guidelines are focused on child sexual abuse, the principles also are applicable to conversing with children about physical abuse as well as exposure to any risk factor, including domestic violence, parental drug and alcohol abuse, neglect, and witnessing a crime.

Ideally, the interviewer works in a multidisciplinary context in order to gather details needed by many different professionals who ultimately will evaluate the child's statements (law enforcement, child protection workers, attorneys, and treatment providers). Child interviewers must constantly balance the interlocking and sometimes competing goals of thorough and uncontaminated fact-gathering, long-term child protection issues, and the child's current emotional well-being.

Although the guidelines represent ideas regarding best practice, they are not intended as a standard of practice and they are not currently endorsed by any professional or legal entity. The guidelines were developed via a thorough literature review, and, where research was unavailable or inconclusive, the collected clinical experience of the authors. Because child interviewing is part art and part science, there is no clear definition of a "perfect" interview. It is essential that evaluators have the freedom to exercise clinical judgment in individual cases. Child interviewers should be knowledgeable regarding the literature on child interviewing and should be prepared to justify their decisions in individual cases.

It is hoped that these guidelines will function as a working document, to be periodically updated as scientific knowledge about child interviewing expands.

❑ Flow of the Interview

The interview can be divided into three phases, each with particular goals and predictable pitfalls. In the beginning phase, the child is acclimated to the setting and task. The middle phase focuses on questioning, whereas the end phase permits the child to seek resolution.[1]

As an interview begins, the child and the interviewer are forging a relationship, and the child is likely making a decision regarding his or her ability to trust this interviewer with sensitive information. The interviewer needs to create an atmosphere of acceptance and understanding, while simultaneously emphasizing the seriousness of the task. The interviewer may want to assess the child's acquisition of forensically relevant concepts (counting, time), and the child's language abilities. The interviewer also will be acquainting the child with the question-and-answer format and setting up expectations that the interviewer is listening carefully to the child's responses and is taking the child's statements seriously. The goals of the beginning phase thus include rapport building, developmental assessment, and task definition.

Once the stage has been set, the interviewer can move the child into the abuse-questioning phase. The focus during this portion of the interview is on posing careful, nonleading questions and on eliciting a complete account from the child regarding any abusive events. The interviewer should use information gained in the initial portion of the interview to gauge the complexity of the language used and the type of questions asked (e.g., not asking about the number of incidents if the child cannot count or manipulate numbers). The interviewer may also want to use this time to check on exposure to risk factors such as drug use, domestic violence, and pornographic materials. Although this portion of the interview is very task-focused, it is recommended that the interviewer remain sensitive to the child's emotional needs and be willing to digress from the task if necessary. The interviewer will be relying on rapport developed in the early phases as an emotional anchor for the child, and as a clinical guide in gauging when to press an issue and when to allow the child to avoid or distract from the questioning. Thus, the questioning phase requires both a high level of clinical acumen and a thorough understanding of forensic issues.

Once the interviewer decides to terminate the interview (either because all available information has been gathered or because a decision has been made to continue at a later date), it is important to allow the child to achieve closure and at least a temporary emotional resolution. During the closure phase, the interviewer can commend the child for his or her cooperation and should give the child the opportunity to ask the interviewer questions about the process. It is also a good time to allow the child to express worries or fears regarding the disclosure or the investigative process. This last section is focused more on the child's emotional needs than on gathering information, although the interviewer must continue to avoid statements or behaviors that might contaminate the child's future reports. Finally, the interviewer should engage the child in a discussion of lighter topics, to ease the transition out of the room.

The information presented in this document will be ordered to correspond to the phases of the interview. That is, issues pertinent to the early phases or throughout the interview will be presented first, with questioning phase issues next, and recommendations for closure at the end.

❏ Guideline List

CHILD ELIGIBILITY FOR A FORENSIC INTERVIEW

Children making statements regarding possible abuse should be provided the opportunity to participate in a forensic interview with a well-trained professional. Decisions about whether to forensically interview other children who are at risk for possible abuse vary according to whether the local evaluation center subscribes to a medical model or an advocacy center model, and according to local legal climates and multidisciplinary team decisions regarding the best approach to at-risk children.

INTERVIEWER TRAINING

Child abuse interviewers should have several years' experience working with children and a background in mental health, child protection, or law enforcement.

Critical supplements to the interviewer's background training include (a) review of literature on children's emotional, cognitive, and linguistic development; (b) training in techniques for assessing children's legal and linguistic competence and for eliciting statements from children using non-leading questions and interviewing tools; and (c) background information on the dynamics of child abuse and its impact on children. Continuing education in the form of peer consultation, literature updates, and legal updates also will be essential.

MULTIDISCIPLINARY TEAM INVOLVEMENT

It is the duty of the county multidisciplinary team (MDT) to ensure that child abuse evaluations are conducted in the most efficient and effective manner possible. MDT roles vary from county to county and include triage for and participation in individual child evaluations, as well as oversight and case consultation for evaluation centers.

ESTABLISHING A NEUTRAL ENVIRONMENT

The interview setting should be childproofed and decorated like a living room or playroom with children's art and comfortable, simple, appropriately sized furniture. Light, temperature, and odor should be pleasant and unobtrusive. The interview setting should be removed from the context of abuse, and every effort should be made to ensure that biased adults do not influence the child during the evaluation.

SINGLE VERSUS MULTIPLE INTERVIEWERS

The number of people questioning a child about possible abuse should be minimized. Whenever possible, one professional interviewer should gather all of the relevant information from the child, with multiple sessions scheduled in complex cases or when new information arises.

FRIENDLY, NEUTRAL APPROACH TO CHILDREN

The interviewer's demeanor with the child and the child's caregivers should be calm, warm, and welcoming. The interviewer must assume the role of a neutral information gatherer and should work to avoid preconceptions regarding whether the child was or was not abused. This approach will strengthen the interview by putting the child and the parent at ease and encouraging their trust in the interviewer.

GATHERING AND DOCUMENTING
THE BACKGROUND INFORMATION

The type of information gathered depends upon the purposes of the evaluation. Information likely to be important for any child interviewer includes descriptions of prior interviews, sources of sexual knowledge, and current experience with nonabusive genital touch (e.g., bathing, toileting, and genital exams at the doctor's office).

SETTING THE STAGE

Young children possess limited knowledge of the task demands in the forensic interview, including the kinds of information and the level of detail they are expected to report. Interviewers must be prepared to orient the child to expected roles for child and interviewer, rules of communication, and the reasons for the interview.

POSING APPROPRIATE QUESTIONS

The interviewer should elicit as much information as possible utilizing open-ended questions that encourage the child to produce a free-running narrative. When necessary to ensure clarity, the interviewer can move along a continuum of questions (Faller, 1990a) from general to specific, using discretion in selecting questions that elicit accurate information and facilitate complete disclosure.

THE USE OF LANGUAGE IN CHILD INTERVIEWS

The interviewer should utilize simple words and short sentences when questioning children regarding possible sexual abuse. With children under the age of 6, the interviewer must be particularly mindful of possible linguistic limitations.

THE USE OF REPEATED QUESTIONS IN CHILD INTERVIEWS

Once a child has responded to an interviewer's question, the same question should not be repeated.

USING ANATOMICAL DOLLS AND OTHER TOOLS

Anatomical dolls and drawings and simple figure drawings are useful tools for interviewing suspected child abuse victims. Such props are most helpful when used as anatomical models and demonstration aids. Their use as cues to stimulate recall is more controversial.

ENDING THE INTERVIEW

Once all available information has been gathered, the interviewer should give the child the opportunity to ask questions and should make an effort to end the interview on a positive note.

MEMORY AND SUGGESTIBILITY

Children perceive, remember, and report events differently than do adults. Fundamentally, the interviewer's task is to cue the child's memory without tainting the memory or adversely impacting the way it is reported.

INACCURATE OR FALSE REPORTS

When an interviewer or other multidisciplinary team member is concerned that a child is making a false report, the interviewer should ask clarifying questions, so long as the questioning process will not be unduly stressful to the child.

THE NONDISCLOSING CHILD

Nondisclosure is an acceptable and likely outcome to many child abuse interviews. There are many possible reasons for nondisclosure in a given interview. When there is a concern regarding barriers to disclosure, the interviewer must assess the child's ability to handle sensitive clarifying questions.

INTERVIEWING THE SPECIAL NEEDS CHILD

When a child with special needs must be evaluated for possible sexual abuse, the interviewer should prepare in advance to minimize the accommodations the child must make in the interview setting. The interviewer should acquire information from people familiar with the child to answer the following questions:

1. What is the special need?
2. How does the special need affect the child in normal situations (school)?
3. How will the special need affect the child's participation in the interview?

COPING WITH CUSTODY AND VISITATION DISPUTES

Evaluating allegations of child sexual abuse in the context of custody and visitation disputes can be especially challenging and time-consuming. The interviewer should allow extra time for these evaluations and should be cautious in making contact and visitation recommendations.

❑ **Note**

1. There is some controversy regarding the activities within different phases, and several areas have been the focus of intense research. These issues will be addressed in the body of the manual.

PART I

Getting Ready

1

Child Eligibility
for a Forensic Interview

❑ **Guideline**

Children making statements regarding possible abuse should be provided the opportunity to participate in a forensic interview with a well-trained professional. Decisions about whether to forensically interview other children who are at risk for possible abuse vary according to whether the local evaluation center subscribes to a medical model or to an advocacy center model and also vary according to local legal climates and multidisciplinary team decisions regarding the best approach to at-risk children.

❑ **Supporting Information**

1. TWO MODELS OF CHILD ABUSE EVALUATION

On a national level, there are two models of child abuse evaluation, each with different affiliations, different historical roots, and different assumptions regarding how to conduct the best possible evaluation of suspected abuse. In some communities, one model is prevalent, whereas in others, the two models are blended. It is important to note that although the models are distinct, the conduct of the forensic interview within each model is virtually identical.

Generally, the **medical model** centers on a medical examination. This model originated on the West Coast, with centers in Denver, Colorado; San Diego, California; Seattle, Washington; and Portland, Oregon. Commonly, the interviewer is a social worker or other mental health professional employed as part of a team that includes pediatric specialists. Most children who come to the center receive a medical examination, unless the exam has been completed by another competent medical provider. Some children are interviewed exclusively within the context of the medical examination, whereas other children participate in a separate forensic interview. Proponents of this model typically assume that the exam is important in every case, because children may not disclose the full extent of their abuse, especially initially. Moreover, the symptoms of sexually transmitted diseases may be quite subtle and may not be detected without medical evaluation. This model emphasizes the child's overall health, as well as concerns specific to the child's allegations. Because of the doctor's socially sanctioned role as a healer, the medical context is thought to promote truthful reporting of symptoms and problems. In addition, the experience of the anogenital exam may cue the child's memory so that the exam process facilitates child disclosure. The medical exception to the hearsay rule may be used in court to facilitate admission of the child's statements during the medical examination and during any associated forensic interviews.

The **advocacy center** model emphasizes the child interview. This model originated on the East Coast, with the most prominent center being in Huntsville, Alabama. These programs are frequently associated with the local district attorney's office, and center employees may be paid by the district attorney. Some advocacy centers employ their own child interviewers, whereas others use experienced law enforcement and child protection workers who come to the center to do the interview but otherwise are employed by other agencies.

In this way, the advocacy center model makes use of existing expertise. Frequently, this model focuses on the child's statements, and
medical evaluations may be requested only for those children alleging penetration or who are displaying concerning symptoms. Medical examinations may be used on a limited basis because of (a) the
belief that anogenital exams can be invasive, and because (b) few
children have abnormal examinations or sexually transmitted diseases. In many communities medical personnel contract with the
center to do exams on an as needed basis and are not employed by
the center. Proponents of the advocacy center model view the evaluation as essentially forensic in nature and would consider components of the evaluation that are not directly related to the allegation
to represent psychosocial or medical assessment. Advocacy center
guidelines recommend that these evaluation components not be
included in the advocacy center casefile (Sorenson, Bottoms, &
Perona, 1997). Frequently, legal proceedings are also conducted at
the advocacy center. Grand jury hearings may occur in this context,
and meetings with court-appointed special advocates (CASA) may
also occur at the center. The child and family gain familiarity with
the center during the forensic interview, and it is believed that the
court proceedings are less stressful to the child and family because
they occur in a familiar setting.

Both advocacy center and medical model programs at times are
affiliated with a treatment component, to assist the child and family
with mental health follow-up following the evaluation.

2. ELIGIBILITY FOR A FORENSIC INTERVIEW

Overall, advocacy center programs and medical model programs
would likely agree to evaluate a partially overlapping group of
children. However, there are some children who would be considered for evaluation within a medical program yet would not typically be seen for a forensic interview in an advocacy center. For
example, a medical program will likely provide an examination and
possible interview to a child whose symptoms are exclusively physical, such as anogenital or pelvic pain, bleeding, or discharge. These
children would be seen because the medical evaluators are special-

ists in pediatric gynecology and are in the best position to render an accurate differential diagnosis, including evaluating the likelihood that the child's symptoms are related to possible sexual abuse. An advocacy center may not see these children until they are diagnosed with a sexually transmitted disease or until the medical provider determines there is good reason to suspect sexual abuse.

Likewise, some children would be interviewed under the advocacy center model, who might be excluded from evaluation at a medical center. For example, the National Children's Advocacy Center handbook (Sorenson, Bottoms, & Perona, 1997) clearly states that children who have witnessed crimes or been kidnapped might be interviewed at the advocacy center. In jurisdictions with medical model programs, these children would likely be interviewed by the police or social service agencies.

> *Most medical model and advocacy center programs require notification of investigative entities.*

Across medical model and advocacy center programs, there is also variability according to local multidisciplinary team decisions and local legal climates regarding which cases will be evaluated. For example, some centers only accept referrals from law enforcement or social service agencies. Other centers accept referrals from pediatricians, therapists, and parents. Most centers do require notification of investigative entities (law enforcement, social services agencies), irrespective of the initial referral source. Also, as noted earlier, some programs have partially blended medical assessment and advocacy center models, borrowing components of each model.

It is hoped that this discussion proves it is not possible to write guidelines for selection of cases that would apply to all centers. However, it is possible to suggest that one group of children could benefit from a full forensic interview regarding possible abuse. Verbal children aged 3 to 18 who meet the following criteria should be considered for a forensic interview, within both the medical and advocacy center models:

- The child is making statements of physical or sexual abuse.
- The child has been witnessed being abused.

- The child lives in a risky environment (lives with an accused or convicted perpetrator, a sibling discloses abuse, the parent is not protective).
- The child has documented anogenital injuries, with or without a disclosure of abuse.
- The child is pregnant or has been diagnosed with a sexually transmitted disease (unless the child is teenaged and is alleging consensual intercourse with a partner whose age does not meet the criteria for statutory rape).
- The child is exhibiting highly sexualized behavior.

We recommend only that these children be **considered** for evaluation, because some of these criteria are controversial as well. For example, some centers do not interview children under age 4. Others do not believe it is helpful to conduct a forensic interview when there is sexualized behavior or a concern of statutory rape with a teenager. In each of these situations, there are provisions made to evaluate the children (a medical exam for children under 4, a mental health evaluation for children with sexualized behavior and statutory rape cases), but there is controversy regarding the utility of a **forensic** interview.

3. CASE PRIORITIZATION

Decisions regarding case priority and which children to see on an emergency basis will vary across medical and advocacy models and within different legal jurisdictions. Medical model programs would typically agree to emergency evaluations of children making disclosures within 72 hours of the alleged abuse, due to concerns regarding potential deterioration of medical and forensic evidence after the 72-hour period. Advocacy center models would likely evaluate these children on a non-emergency basis, once the medical evaluation is complete.

Advocacy center models would consider children living with an alleged offender, children with unsupportive families, and children who have been threatened to be eligible for emergency evaluation (Sorenson, Bottoms, & Perona, 1997). Medical model programs might evaluate these children on an emergency basis or might rely on social services workers to intervene initially and schedule the child for the first available evaluation appointment. In addition, advocacy center programs would prioritize cases in which the offender is in custody, the offender is a flight risk, there are allegations of child pornography, or there are multiple victims. Medical model programs might prioritize these cases but also might rely on law enforcement to do screening interviews and conduct initial investigations prior to the medical evaluation. Decisions regarding case prioritization are generally made in consultation with local multidisciplinary teams that include the center director as well as representatives from law enforcement and social service agencies.

4. FLOW OF AN EVALUATION

Once a child has been accepted for evaluation, it is helpful for center staff to help the child's caretaker prepare the child for the evaluation (Sorenson, Bottoms, & Perona, 1997). The caretakers should be discouraged from discussing the allegation with their child prior to the evaluation. However, they should be encouraged to provide emotional support if the child broaches the topic (e.g., hugs, reassurances). It is helpful for the child to have a general understanding of the purpose of the evaluation (e.g., "to make sure you are safe and healthy," "to talk to you about the things you told your teacher"). The child should be encouraged to tell the truth and should be reassured that (a) the caretaker will support him or her during the evaluation, and (b) the evaluation center staff are supportive and friendly.

Caretakers should be discouraged from discussing allegations with their child prior to an evaluation.

Generally, the family is greeted by support staff and completes intake paperwork. It is helpful if the child and caretakers are shown the examination and/or interview rooms prior to the evaluation. The process of showing the rooms permits rapport development between the interviewer and the child's caretakers and may reduce both caretaker and child anxiety, because the setting of the evaluation is known and appears inviting and comfortable. Rapport that is developed between the interviewer and caretakers can assist the child in conversing with the interviewer, because the child may feel that his or her caretaker is comfortable with the interviewer and supports the evaluation. Discussions of the allegation should be carefully avoided at this point.

In some centers, the child's caretakers are extensively interviewed, whereas in other programs the caretakers are briefly interviewed or not interviewed at all prior to the child's evaluation (for more information on this topic, see Chapter 7, "Gathering and Documenting Background Information"). The child is greeted by the evaluator and may be interviewed first, then examined, or examined first and then interviewed, again depending on the program guidelines. The interviewer and/or examiner may consult with multidisciplinary team members during the child's evaluation.

Following the child's evaluation, the interviewer may consult with other professionals attending the evaluation. Decisions are made regarding what to say to the family about the child's statements and what the level of law enforcement and social service agency involvement is likely to be. The interviewer then meets with the parents, sometimes with other professionals present in the room. At times, the family will meet with professionals who will be responsible for investigative or mental health follow-up after their discussions with the interviewer. For example, court appointed special advocates, law enforcement officers, social service agencies, and mental health consultants may meet with the family to begin the process of investigating the allegation or providing services to the child and/or family.

Some centers document the evaluation via extensive reports and/or videotapes of the child's interview. Other centers utilize intake paperwork and interview notes or audio/videotapes as the only documentation for the evaluation. Please see Chapter 14, "Verbatim Documentation," for more details on this topic and for recommendations on how to document forensic interviews.

2

Interviewer Training

❑ **Guideline**

Child abuse interviewers should have several years' experience working with children and a background in mental health, child protection, or law enforcement.

Critical supplements to the interviewer's background training include (a) review of literature on children's emotional, cognitive, and linguistic development; (b) training in techniques for assessing children's legal and linguistic competence and for eliciting statements from children using non-leading questions and interviewing tools; and (c) background information on the dynamics of child abuse and its impact on children. Continuing education in the form of peer consultation, literature updates, and legal updates also will be essential.

❏ **Supporting Information**

1. SKILL IN SPEAKING WITH CHILDREN
   IS OF PRIMARY IMPORTANCE

As children grow and develop, they pass through stages in which their language skills, reasoning abilities, and behavior patterns are unique to their age group. Within an age group, there is tremendous variability in children's abilities to report past events. These developmental phases and individual variability within phases present child interviewers with both an opportunity and a challenge. The skilled child interviewer has the opportunity to facilitate communication with the child at his or her highest functional level. The challenge is to be sufficiently well trained in child development and sufficiently experienced in conversing with children that the child's communication is facilitated. The interviewer should possess skills in conversing with children as a prerequisite to being hired.

The skilled child interviewer has the opportunity to facilitate communication with the child.

Studies show that persons such as child counselors and schoolteachers (Brennan & Brennan, 1988) are very good at asking questions that children are able to comprehend and answer. Probably because comprehension barriers are removed, the accuracy of information given to these groups is typically greater, with fewer errors. Other individuals who have their own children or who have high levels of professional experience with children (e.g., certain law enforcement officers and child protection workers) are also likely to possess the requisite ease in questioning and responding to children. These skills are more important, and likely a more reliable indicator of interviewer potential, than possessing particular professional degrees.

2. TWO DOMAINS OF TRAINING:
CHILD DEVELOPMENT AND FORENSIC PRACTICE

Research suggests that when child interviewing specialists are knowledgeable about child development and are trained in forensic issues (e.g., using open-ended versus leading questions), more accurate information is elicited, and system-induced stress to children is reduced (California Attorney General's Office, 1994). In addition, access to mental health services is generally improved.

3. FOCUSED TRAINING WILL BE NECESSARY

Training in basic child development, the dynamics of abuse, and specific forensic interviewing skills permits the interviewer to conduct a competent assessment of the abuse allegation. Thus, interviewers must have a basic knowledge of the following areas:

- Current scientific literature regarding child interviews
- The basic literature on child development
- The dynamics of child abuse and the impact of abuse on children

Regarding forensic child interviewing, the trainee should be exposed to basic material on conducting a developmentally appropriate assessment of a young child's linguistic and legal competence; procedures to maintain interviewer neutrality; definitions of question types and how to use them; information on the use of anatomical dolls and other tools; interviewing techniques that minimize the occurrence of false allegations, recantation, and denial; and information on child memory and suggestibility. Relevant summaries of this material are contained in the current volume. A summary of primary sources for information about forensic child interviews is included in Appendix A.

If the interviewer will be testifying in court, background reading, the viewing of trials in progress, and practice with experienced testifiers and/or the attorney calling the interviewer as a witness are all quite valuable introductions to the courtroom environment. Suggested background readings include Stern (1997) and Melton, Petrila, Poythress, & Slobogin (1987).

In addition to specific knowledge regarding forensic interviewing, the interviewer should have a basic understanding of children's emotional, cognitive, and linguistic development. Anne Walker's (1994) book provides a focused, highly relevant summary of children's linguistic competence. A summary of linguistic issues during a forensic interview for children of different ages also is provided in this volume. A basic knowledge of the development of children's ability to remember and to report events is critical to questioning children and to understanding their answers. A summary of these issues is provided in this volume. Other excellent sources include Ceci and Bruck's (1993) article and Fivush's chapter in Goodman and Bottom's (1993) book. Knowledge of children's emotional development can be garnered from undergraduate or graduate coursework or from reading a basic text such as Brazelton's (1992). Steward, Bussey, Goodman, and Saywitz's (1993) article also is highly relevant. It is most important that the interviewer garner an understanding of the critical nature of the child's attachment relationship with primary caregivers and the implications this relationship has for reporting abuse at different ages.

To competently interpret a child's behavior and statements during an evaluation for possible abuse, the interviewer should be exposed to literature on the dynamics of child abuse, the impact of child sexual abuse on children, and cultural issues related to child maltreatment. The writings of Sorensen and Snow (1991), Summit (1983), Finkelhor and Brown (1985), and Kendall-Tackett, Williams, and Finkelhor (1993) provide an excellent introduction to the topics of abuse dynamics and the impact of abuse on children. Fontes's (1995) book is a good introduction to issues of cultural competence.

It is helpful for the interviewer to maintain a basic knowledge of medical findings regarding child abuse and current scientific literature regarding offender behavior. The interviewer must work well in a team setting and be able to seek feedback from other interviewers, law enforcement, and child protection staff regarding the types of information important to their work.

4. INITIAL TRAINING INCLUDES LITERATURE
REVIEW AND APPRENTICESHIP

Ideally, centers that utilize child interviewers would maintain a collection of articles and books that represent important historical articles, research summaries, and current findings regarding interviewing practice. For a suggested list of materials based on the current literature, see Appendix A.

Persons new to the field of child interviewing should be provided with a one- to two-month training period, depending upon their background qualifications. During that time, the prospective interviewer should review the agency's collection of literature and receive "hands-on" interviewing instruction with careful supervision. The trainee should observe and critique interviews by experienced interviewers and should look for opportunities to practice interviewing skills. For example, role playing with experienced interviewers and conversing with children about innocuous events provide excellent practice opportunities. The American Professional Society on the Abuse of Children (APSAC) and several other organizations also are offering hands-on intensive training institutes for child interviewers, which do involve role play and the practice of both basic and advanced interviewing skills. Experienced child interviewers may require only an orientation to the center's approach and assistance in locating relevant research articles and continuing education opportunities.

There are many different training models for hands-on experience. One method known as **cognitive apprenticeship** is available and, although not labeled as such, provides an accurate description of good training practices found in many child abuse centers (Collins, Brown, & Hollum, 1991). Cognitive apprenticeship is built upon the premise that retention of information is strongly enhanced when the learner is an active participant rather than a passive observer during the training process. Portions of the cognitive apprenticeship model could be used to assist both new interviewers and experienced interviewers looking to sharpen their skills.

Cognitive apprenticeship consists of six stages of learning/ teaching:

A. Modeling: An expert performs the task, and learners observe. When no local expert is available, videotapes of experts can be viewed. Ideally, interviewers would view experts who were also available for consultation so that questions could be addressed and the experts could expose their reasoning process for decisions made during the interview.

B. Coaching: Learners attempt the task, and an expert offers feedback aimed at bringing their performance closer to expert levels. This, too, could be accomplished via videotape review, with expert consultation.

C. Scaffolding: The expert constructively, but accurately, diagnoses the learner's current skill level and deficits to be addressed. The expert then offers support to the learner to increase his or her skill level (literature review, modeling of interactions, focused videotape review, having the learner take on portions of the evaluation to learn one thing at a time, putting the expert behind the mirror, or using a bug in the ear to provide modeling during the assessment). In the final stages of scaffolding, supports are faded until the learners function independently.

D. Articulation: Learners and experts verbalize their reasoning abilities, problem-solving processes, and sources of knowledge brought to bear on a particular decision or use of a technique (e.g., "Why did you use the dolls during that assessment?"; "Because I felt the child was anxious, and therefore having trouble focusing, so I thought the dolls would give us a common focus.").

E. Reflection: Learners compare their own problem-solving processes with those of an expert. Reflection is enhanced by replaying (via video or role-play) the performances of the expert and the learner for comparison (e.g., "I agree with your observation that this child needed a focus. However, I don't think I would have used the dolls with this particular child, due to her distractibility. I would have been worried about overstimulating her. I might have tried a drawing instead. How did the dolls work for you with this child? Did they help her focus?").

F. **Exploration:** Learners are encouraged to identify and solve problems independently. General goals are set for learners regarding gaps in skills or challenging issues to address. Learners are encouraged to focus literature review, conference attendance, and supervision on these issues. Learners are encouraged to continually revise their goals and evaluate their performance so that the training process is lifelong and growth-sustaining. In this way, today's learners become tomorrow's experts.

> *The training process is lifelong; today's learners become tomorrow's experts.*

5. CONTINUING EDUCATION INCLUDES PEER CONSULTATION AND LITERATURE REVIEW

In the area of child abuse interviewing, **peer consultation** is essential. Depending upon the center's volume of interviewing, peer consultation can be accomplished weekly, monthly, or on an "as needed" basis for difficult cases. Centers should be willing to make their experienced interviewers available for consultation with less experienced interviewers, both within the center and across centers in the same geographical area. Peer consultation permits ongoing cognitive apprenticeship and provides emotional support to child interviewers, who, by the nature of the work, are at high risk for vicarious traumatization. See the following section for a summary of the need to protect the child's confidentiality when peer consultation is utilized.

Centers should periodically update their collection of literature on child development and child interviewing. Annual or every other year attendance at **conferences** (indexed to the individual interviewer's case load) and maintenance of **subscriptions** to relevant journals should be sufficient in this domain. Interviewers who attend a conference should share the knowledge gained, along with relevant articles, with other interviewers in the same center.

Consultation with multidisciplinary team members (the child protection and law enforcement persons who attend the evaluation), and with attorneys when a case goes to court, is very helpful in updating understanding of the legal context. Following an interview, or a court appearance, the interviewer should solicit feedback and suggestions for improvement.

6. INFORMED CONSENT FOR PEER CONSULTATION

Unless peers are part of the evaluation process, peer consultation represents a potential violation of the child's right to confidentiality. Yet during an evaluation for possible abuse, the right to confidentiality is frequently at least partially waived due to the need for investigative agencies to share information. Moreover, in some settings peer consultation that occurs under the auspices of quality assurance protocols is not considered a violation of confidentiality. The laws governing the child's and parent's rights to confidentiality and to informed consent for release of records will vary according to the geographical location of the evaluation and according to whether the evaluation occurs in a medical center or an advocacy center. Views on ethical obligations to the child also may vary across professional lines (police, social work, medicine, and psychology). It is not possible to make a definitive statement regarding center policy for permitting peer consultation. At a minimum, centers should have in place a consent form acknowledging that peer consultation occurs and that it is used as a mechanism for ensuring that professionals evaluating the child maintain their expertise. By signing the form, the child's legal guardian acknowledges an understanding of the need for consultation and gives permission for the child to be evaluated under the condition that the tape may be shown to other professionals. It also may be helpful in the consent form to detail the mechanisms for protecting the child's identity when the tapes are shown to other professionals (e.g., the child's name will be deleted).

❏   *Practice Tips*   ❏

1. Court preparation offers the opportunity for focused literature updates

Frequently, in consulting with attorneys prior to a court appearance, focal issues will be identified. The interviewer can examine the center's collection of literature and/or consult with expert interviewers in the same geographical region for suggested literature citations to address these issues.

2. Journal clubs can facilitate literature review

The journal club is a regular (once a week, once a month) brief meeting in which members review a piece of literature prior to the meeting and discuss it at the meeting. The club could include members from different centers that are geographically proximate.

3. Note cards summarizing findings and critiques are helpful memory aids

When an interviewer reviews an article, a brief summary, along with critiques, can be stored in a card file along with references. The interviewer can use the note card as a quick refresher before court. The notes also give guidance to other interviewers during their literature searches.

3

Multidisciplinary Team Involvement

❏ **Guideline**

It is the duty of the county multidisciplinary team (MDT) to ensure that child abuse evaluations are conducted in the most efficient and effective manner possible. MDT roles vary from county to county and include triage for and participation in individual child evaluations, as well as oversight and case consultation for evaluation centers.

❏ **Supporting Information**

1. WHO PARTICIPATES IN THE MULTIDISCIPLINARY TEAM?

There are generally two levels of MDT participation. Typically, representatives from the district attorney's office, law enforcement, child protective services, and evaluation center directors are **county MDT** members. This MDT maintains communication between investigative agencies and center managers regarding the center's integration into the larger system. This group is also typically available for consultation on difficult or problematic cases.

On the day of the evaluation, a **case-specific MDT** ideally will gather to participate in the child's evaluation. This team will typically consist of individuals assigned to work with this child and family and may include the law enforcement officer assigned to the case, any child protection caseworkers who have been assigned to work with the child and family, the physician who conducted the sexual abuse exam, the child's therapist or a consulting therapist, the child's victim's advocate, district attorneys, and the child interviewer. Centers have established different rules regarding who may participate. These rules vary according to the type of center (e.g., medical center versus advocacy center) and according to differing views regarding the importance of neutrality among team members. The National Children's Advocacy Center handbook (Sorenson, Bottoms, & Perona, 1997) suggests that only individuals involved in the investigation be permitted to observe the interview. Investigative entities would likely include the designated interviewer, the assigned law enforcement officer and social services caseworker, and the prosecuting attorney. This handbook also makes provisions for including trainees and researchers, so long as these individuals sign confidentiality statements. Some centers disallow participation of attorneys and therapists because of the advocacy inherent in the professional roles of the two latter groups and the perception that the neutrality of the evaluation might be compromised by their participation. Other centers support inclusion of these professionals because of the assistance they can provide in framing questions and supporting the child. Medical centers would typically include as an observer the medical person who examined the child for possible abuse. Each of these approaches is grounded in theory, and there are currently no data available to discriminate the relative merits of including and excluding particular observers.

2. THE ROLE OF THE INTERVIEWER IN THE MULTIDISCIPLINARY TEAM CONTEXT

Consistently, the role of the interviewer is to converse with the child; to ensure complete, neutral fact-finding; and to document all findings. The interviewer consults with other team members who may need particular pieces of information from the child's interview, so that they can work effectively with the child, family, or perpetrator. The interviewer relies upon the expertise of these professionals, who may understand the importance of a particular piece of information to the long-term outcome (prosecution, child protection) in a way that is not immediately obvious to the interviewer.

The interviewer may act as a liaison between the child and case-specific MDT members. The interviewer should be highly trained regarding child development and regarding appropriate forensic questioning. The interviewer can advise the team when a child is fatigued and when a child cannot answer a question due to developmental considerations. The interviewer also can advise regarding the best approach to addressing difficult questions in a non-leading fashion.

> *The interviewer may act as an educator to the county multidisciplinary team.*

The interviewer also may act as an educator to the county MDT by appearing at case consultations and by appearing in court as an expert witness.

3. WHEN LAW ENFORCEMENT AND/OR CHILD PROTECTION WORKERS INTERVIEW THE CHILD

In some centers, the ongoing multidisciplinary team nominates skilled personnel from law enforcement and/or child protective services to go to the center and do child interviews. At times, these individuals also function in ongoing caseworker and detective roles with the child or family. This approach is particularly effective in smaller communities, or when a center is just becoming established, because it takes advantage of existing expertise.

In these cases, the county MDT overseer role is especially important. The county MDT should strive to reduce the number of persons
conducting child abuse interviews by identifying those who are
most expert in talking with children. These individuals should meet
the training requirements outlined in the "Interviewer Training"
chapter of these guidelines and should be required to master the
literature on child interviewing (summarized in these guidelines).
In addition, the MDT should make a commitment to facilitate ongoing training for these individuals so that they can remain up to date
on current child abuse and child development literature. The intensity of the training requirements leads to the suggestion that the
MDT reduce the number of interviewers to a manageable level.

The center director, in consultation with the county MDT, should
have the final say over who practices interviewing in the center.

4. WHEN LAW ENFORCEMENT OFFICERS
ACT AS OBSERVERS

Law enforcement officers, especially detectives, tend to be involved in a case on an ongoing basis, perhaps all the way through
the trial process. As such, they offer valuable insights regarding
concerns that are likely to arise in court regarding child credibility
and details that may be essential to the investigation. Moreover, law
enforcement officers work constantly within the local legal community, are likely to know the practices of judges and district attorneys,
and are likely to be attuned to local variability in the application of
child abuse laws. Because of these special skills, the law enforcement
officer can direct an interviewer's attention to sources of skepticism
and forensic details that might otherwise be missed by a person with
a mental health background. In addition, by being present at the
interview, the law enforcement officer can assist if there is a need to
assume protective custody, and the officer may be able to expedite
the legal process by arresting the offender on the basis of evidence
contained in the interview. The interview may also assist law enforcement staff in investigating the case, particularly in talking with
the alleged perpetrator.

5. WHEN CHILD PROTECTION WORKERS
   ACT AS OBSERVERS

The child's caseworker must make decisions regarding placement, child safety in the home, and the protective capacities of nonoffending parents. As such, child protection personnel may direct the interviewer's attention to information regarding family dynamics, attachment to the parents, and exposure to risk factors such as domestic violence, drug and alcohol abuse, physical abuse, and neglect. Child protection workers are typically acutely aware of the laws governing foster care placement and can advise the interviewer regarding questions to determine if placement is necessary and what placement options might be available (e.g., asking the child about relationships with extended family members). The caseworker also may be privy to family information that will shed interpretive light on the child's statements and can direct the interviewer to question family members about these issues (e.g., as when a mother has a history of neglect referrals, and the caseworker suggests asking how the child gets food, who provides clothing, etc.).

6. OTHER OBSERVERS

Multidisciplinary collaboration in a child's evaluation is still an experimental concept. As such, counties and centers are free to create their own rules regarding participation, so long as these are consistent with local laws and with the overall goals of the county MDT.

Observers of different professions may make unique contributions to the evaluation. For example, medical observers can be helpful in reminding the interviewer to query regarding penetration, ejaculation, pain, bleeding, and other health concerns. These questions help the medical provider decide what tests to perform and what treatments to offer, and they permit a determination regarding the fit between exam findings and child statements. District attorneys may desire involvement to remind the interviewer to query regarding issues that are likely to arise in court and to more accurately determine the advisability of prosecution. In other countries (e.g., Britain), defense attorneys also participate, so that the child's videotaped interview might substitute for courtroom testimony. Therapists can provide consultation regarding a child's developmental limitations, idiosyncratic communication, and offender issues when there is sexually reactive behavior. The expertise of the therapist can also be utilized to individually tailor both the questioning approach and the methods used to help the child feel safe and supported.

On the other hand, in some communities, medical staff are not available to consult on every case. As was mentioned earlier, the professional roles of therapists and attorneys mandate advocacy on behalf of their clients, and some individuals consider their inclusion to represent a compromise to the neutrality of the evaluation. Moreover, inclusion of individuals other than those mandated by law to investigate the concern of child abuse may represent a violation of the child's and family's confidentiality. Certainly, if individuals with no investigative mandate are to be included as observers, the parents (and possibly the child) should be made aware of their involvement and should be asked to provide consent. As centers and local communities experiment, it is likely that information regarding effective and ineffective practices will emerge and be disseminated.

If individuals with no investigative mandate are to be observers, the parents should be made aware of their involvement and asked to provide consent.

4

Establishing a
Neutral Environment

❑ Guideline

The interview setting should be childproofed and decorated like a living room or playroom with children's art and comfortable, simple, appropriately sized furniture. Light, temperature, and odor should be pleasant and unobtrusive. The interview setting should be removed from the context of abuse, and every effort should be made to ensure that biased adults do not influence the child during the evaluation.

❑ Supporting Information

1. THE AMOUNT AND QUALITY OF INFORMATION OBTAINED IS DIRECTLY RELATED TO THE SETTING

The environment, including the interviewer, other adults present, and the physical setting, influences the amount and quality of the information a child is willing to disclose. Numerous basic research studies suggest that supportive environments are conducive to accurate recall. Moreover, stress interferes with recall, which is in turn associated with heightened suggestibility (cf., Hill & Hill, 1987; Saywitz & Nathanson, 1993). Providing the child with an opportunity to converse in a safe, neutral, child-centered environment minimizes the possibility of further stress to the child, maximizes the quality and quantity of information, reduces the operation of contaminating influences, and thereby maintains the integrity of the interview (Yuille, Hunter, Joffe, & Zaparniuk, 1993).

2. PHYSICAL COMPONENTS OF A NEUTRAL ENVIRONMENT

The following suggestions are drawn from several references, including Large (1995), Sorenson, Bottoms, and Perona (1997), and Batterman-Faunce and Goodman (1993), as well as from our clinical experience.

A. The room is quiet and free from distractions such as the telephone ringing, street noise, and people interrupting. Ideally, the room would be soundproofed, so that the child is not disturbed by overhearing conversations in the hall and worried that his or her conversation might be overheard as well. Carpeting may enhance soundproofing and assists in making the room feel warm and comfortable.

B. The procedure for communication between the interviewer and observers minimizes disruption to the interview process. For example, the interviewer can leave the room during a break or can telephone the observers at a designated time. "Bug in the ear" devices and intercom devices can be unnecessarily disruptive, unless the communication occurs only when interviewers signal that they are available to attend to observers' communications (e.g., the child and/or interviewer are not currently talking).

C. The furniture is comfortable, simple, and appropriately sized. The differing size needs of preschool versus older children can be accommodated either through two separate rooms or through provision of different sizes of furniture in different portions of the same room.

D. The decor is soft and child-friendly—pastel colors, pictures hung at the child's eye level, stuffed animals, and children's art work—conveying the message that other children have been in the room before. Posters and artwork with abuse prevention messages or suggestive images of abuse should not be present in the interviewing room or in any other rooms the child and family are likely to view. The items in the room should not be so numerous as to distract children from the task, however. Paper and crayons or markers provide a neutral activity for engaging most preadolescent (and some adolescent) children. Interviewing tools should not be part of the decor but should be accessible if needed.

E. The temperature should be comfortable.

F. Soft lighting is preferable, though the lighting must be adequate for videotaping.

G. The smell of the room should be pleasant, as opposed to the antiseptic odor of a doctor's office or hospital.

H. The room should be safe, without breakable items, sharp edges, or small parts (which could pose choking hazards to very young children or siblings). Electrical outlets should be covered.

I. Audio/video equipment is unobtrusive (e.g., small microphones are mounted on the wall, cameras or audio recorders are hidden in a cabinet or behind a one-way mirror) but is shown and explained to the child. (Also see Chapter 14, "Verbatim Documentation.")

J. Observers are hidden from the child's view. They may observe or listen to the evaluation via unobtrusive microphones, one-way mirrors, or closed-circuit television.

K. The seating arrangement brings the interviewer to the child's level and is free of objects, such as a table or desk, that would obstruct the space between the child and the interviewer.

L. Facilities to meet a child's basic needs (bathroom and drinking fountains) should be readily accessible but located outside the interview room.

The interview setting should minimize factors that could unwittingly affect the child's statements.

3. THE FACTORS THAT INTIMIDATE A CHILD
   MAY NOT BE KNOWN IN ADVANCE

A police officer in uniform, a physician in a white coat, a nonoffending parent who doubts the allegations, and the school principal's office are a few examples of components that may adversely impact a child. For example, the child may have been taught that the police are "bad" or may find reminders of authority, such as a badge, gun, or radio, intimidating. Other children will find these same symbols of authority comforting. Similarly, some children may experience the principal's office as a place for stern reprimands. The interview setting should minimize factors that could unwittingly affect child statements; the interviewer should be dressed in plain clothes, and the interview room should be made comfortable and soft.

4. THE INTERVIEW SETTING SHOULD BE
   REMOVED FROM THE CONTEXT OF THE ABUSE

Interviewing a child with the alleged offender present may prevent child disclosure. Bussey, Lee, & Ross (1991, April) reported that 3- to 5-year-old children were less likely to report a negative act in the presence of the person who committed the act. Older children (around 9 years old) reported the event in the offender's presence but expressed discomfort in doing so. In a related study, Peters (1991) found that 5- to 10-year-old children were less likely to correctly identify a perpetrator of a theft when faced with a live line-up versus a photo line-up. Many of the children later disclosed to their parents that they knew the correct identification but were too afraid to tell. In both of these studies, the children were reporting witnessed events, versus a personally experienced event such as sexual abuse.

Interviewing a child in the setting in which abuse may have occurred (parent's bedroom, child's bedroom) may also inhibit disclosure. Although contextual cues aid memory retrieval, a child remembering abuse in the same context may become emotionally flooded and unable to provide accurate information.

5. INVOLVEMENT OF OTHER ADULTS IN THE INTERVIEW SHOULD BE DISCOURAGED

The involvement of adults such as nonoffending parents, school personnel, and child caretakers in the interview can inhibit or contaminate the child's disclosure. Many children are sensitive to speaking about abuse with their parents present. Even when parents are supportive, children fear their parents' reactions (anger, sadness, disgust, disbelief). Children are very perceptive (Lawson & Chaffin, 1992). If a child perceives that he will not be believed, that

A child may withhold information to protect himself or those around him.

his caretaker will be unable to handle the disclosures, or if he fears facing an individual after revealing his secret, the child may withhold information to protect himself or those around him.

Supportive adults present during the interview can intentionally or unintentionally coach or nonverbally cue a child, thereby contaminating the interview. For example, children might know that their mothers would like them to make a particular statement and may be more likely to do so if their mothers are present during the evaluation. Likewise, children may have lied or unintentionally misrepresented a fact during a previous interview. The children may be less willing to correct themselves if the individual to whom they made the initial statement is present during the interview. The presence of non-neutral adults in the room may undermine interviewers' efforts to emphasize their own neutrality and their own desire to hear only the truth, in the children's own words. In sum, limiting the number of adults involved in the interview process decreases the operation of outside influences and maintains interview integrity.

6. WHEN A SUPPORTIVE ADULT IS NECESSARY

At times, a child may require a supportive individual's presence. This is particularly likely for very young children with developmentally normal separation anxieties. In these cases, clear instruction should be given to the adult. Specifically, the support person should be told to permit the child to answer in his or her own words and should be instructed to avoid verbal and nonverbal reactions to the child's statements. For example, the interviewer could say: "For us to be able to help your child, we must hear what happened in her own words. We ask that you try not to react in any way to your child's statements. If your child comes to you for support, it is alright for you to comfort her, but please do not offer support unless your child is asking for it." The interviewer may explain that if the support person feels strongly about something the child says, he or she will be given an opportunity to express those sentiments at the completion of the interview, when the child is no longer present.

When a support person is present, it is recommended that he or she be seated close to the child, but out of the child's view, that is, behind the child. The interviewer can begin discussing safe subjects (favorite activities, pets). Once the child appears comfortable, the interviewer can ask the child if it will be alright for the support person to leave. The child can be reassured that the support person will be nearby (and can be shown the location if necessary) and can return at the child's request.

It is a good idea to have the supportive adult tell the child that it is alright for the child to talk openly and freely with the interviewer.

When a supportive adult is present, have him or her tell the child that it is alright to talk openly and freely with the interviewer.

❑ *Practice Tips* ❑

1. Wood or upholstered furniture is warm and friendly

Soft, natural furnishings are preferable to metal or plastic. It should be noted that if upholstered furniture is to be used, a cleaning schedule must be established to prevent disease transmission (lice, scabies) and to keep the furniture appearing new.

2. Scented sachet packets add a pleasant scent to the interview room

3. A balance must be reached between stimulation and distraction

Items such as stuffed animals and quilts add warmth and comfort to a room. Children's toys define a child's space. However, excesses of these items can cause distraction and interfere with the child's ability to focus on questioning. In addition, noisy items should be avoided, because they interfere with monitoring capabilities and adversely affect recording. Many interviewers (Large, 1995) suggest maintaining a larger collection of toys in the waiting area and/or in locked cabinets in the interview room, with a few items, such as one or two stuffed animals and paper with markers, accessible to the child.

4. Use locked cabinets to store interviewing aids

Dolls, drawings, and other materials need to be accessible to the interviewer but out of the child's sight until needed. A small cabinet in the interview room can be an effective storage area for these items. A lock placed on the cabinet can be very helpful in preventing distraction. The key can be kept in the interview room on a hook out of the child's reach.

5. Signage

To minimize outside interruption, it is suggested that signs be placed on the doors of the interview and observation rooms to alert people that an interview is in progress.

6. Snacks and beverages

Offering snacks and beverages to a child is an almost universal means of communicating nurturance, welcoming, and acceptance. Moreover, research indicates that when children are offered snacks by a friendly interviewer, the children are more resistant to leading questions (Goodman, Bottoms, Schwartz-Kenney, & Rudy, 1991). It is important to note that these effects occurred when snacks were offered irrespective of the child's statements during the interview. When treats or snacks are used to ply disclosure from a child or are only given to children who have disclosed, the meaning of the snack changes from a symbol of nurturance to a symbol of coercion. Because food and drink can be distracting and can make it difficult to understand what the child is saying, these items would ideally be offered when the interviewer is first greeting the family, so the child can consume them while background information is being gathered.

5

Single Versus
Multiple Interviewers

❏ **Guideline**

The number of people questioning a child about possible abuse should be minimized. Whenever possible, one professional interviewer should gather all of the relevant information from the child, with multiple sessions scheduled in complex cases or when new information arises.

❏ **Supporting Information**

1. THERE WILL USUALLY BE MORE THAN ONE INTERVIEWER

Typically, when there is a suspicion of sexual abuse, a child will have disclosed to someone (a parent, therapist, school counselor), and that person will need to gather some information in order to protect the child. Child protection workers and/or law enforcement officers may need to gather additional information to provide protection to the child while waiting for the center-based assessment to be scheduled.

Ideally, in these cases, the professional taking the child's statement should decide whether a center-based assessment will be scheduled. If the child is to be evaluated at a center, it is recommended that only minimal information be gathered. Specifically, therapists, counselors, child protection workers, law enforcement officers, and any other persons to whom the child discloses should gather only enough information to substantiate a concern of abuse and to identify the alleged offender so that the child can be protected (e.g., typically "Who" and "What" information). Frequently, this information will be contained in the child's initial disclosure, and no further questioning will be necessary, as when the child says, "Daddy touched my privates." In such cases, the initial interviewer(s) can give the child support and reassure the child that he or she will be protected.

If a center-based assessment is not scheduled, it is recommended that the child be interviewed by a skilled therapist, law enforcement officer, or child protection worker. If one of these individuals also receives the initial disclosure, he or she may function as the child's primary interviewer, and gather all relevant information, even if multiple sessions are needed to address concerns from different disciplines. The designated interviewer should also adhere to the guidelines embodied in this document, whenever possible, particularly regarding verbatim documentation.

2. MINIMIZING THE NUMBER OF INTERVIEWERS REDUCES THE POTENTIAL FOR CONTAMINATION

Van de Kamp (1986) studied children's progression through a police investigation of child abuse and noted that the average child endured seven police interviews. Most children also were interviewed by other individuals such as parents, teachers, and child welfare workers. The likelihood that each of these interviewers will be completely unbiased, as well as skilled at posing appropriate questions, is very low.

3. MINIMIZING THE NUMBER OF INTERVIEWERS REDUCES STRESS TO THE CHILD

When interviewed by multiple persons, the child is required to extend trust regarding a very sensitive topic to numerous individuals who are likely to be relative strangers.

In addition, multiple interviews by different individuals can be needlessly stressful to the child who is feeling embarrassed, ashamed, or fearful of perpetrator retribution.

4. IDEALLY, ALL CONVERSATIONS WITH THE CHILD WOULD BE DOCUMENTED

In order to track potential sources of contamination, all conversations with the child regarding the allegations should be documented, including both questions and answers. Child protection workers and law enforcement officers should carefully document questions and answers, either via recordings or in detailed notes during their conversations with the child. Center personnel should encourage parents, teachers, and other persons receiving the initial disclosure to write notes regarding their conversations with the child.

If prior conversations have not been documented, the center interviewer should document these conversations at the time of the assessment. An attempt should be made to gather information regarding the context of the initial disclosure (spontaneous versus that elicited through questioning), as well as the specific questions and answers. The interviewer can then use this information to detect potential sources of bias and may be able to gear questioning to assess the impact on the child (emotionally and cognitively) of any biased information.

5. THE NEED FOR MULTIPLE SESSIONS IN SOME CASES

Many centers are designed to complete interviews in a single session. Clinical practice reveals that this protocol works for many children. However, some groups of children will require more than one session in order to fully disclose. For example, when children are abused over a long period of time or when there is an ongoing custody battle, the time required to gather complete information may exceed the child's ability to attend to and concentrate on the interviewer's questions. Other children may have difficulty disclosing to a relative stranger. Very young children (Boat & Everson, 1988; Hewitt, 1991) and children with special needs are likely to fall into this latter category. Younger children more often disclose accidentally or are referred due to concerning behaviors, statements, or physical findings (Sorensen & Snow, 1991). It is likely to take less time to elicit information from a child who intentionally discloses than from one who is referred for other reasons.

> *Multiple sessions may be necessary to establish rapport with a child.*

In these instances, multiple sessions may be necessary to establish rapport with the child and thus ease more slowly into abuse-focused questioning. Ideally, centers would develop protocols for deciding when to schedule follow-up interviews. These protocols should also clearly delineate forensic goals of follow-up sessions, to maintain distinctions between the interview situation and more therapeutically driven conversations.

6. MULTIPLE SESSIONS ARE NOT LIKELY TO BE PROBLEMATIC WHEN THEY ARE WELL-DOCUMENTED AND ARE CONDUCTED BY A SINGLE, UNBIASED INTERVIEWER

A large body of research suggests that repeated recall of information may inoculate against forgetting (see Brainerd & Ornstein, 1991, for a review). Multiple recall sessions produce more accurate information than single sessions, and more information is recalled during later sessions than during earlier sessions. Similarly, young children may produce highly accurate reports but may provide very different information across sessions (see Fivush, 1993, for a review). Thus, interviews over multiple sessions may be necessary to elicit complete accounts from some children. Moreover, several writers (see Faller, 1996a, for a review) recommend multiple sessions to conduct a more complete assessment of the child's adjustment rather than focusing primarily on abuse.

Multiple interviews may be beneficial for some children, but only when they are neutral. Neutral interviews (Ceci & Bruck, 1995) are characterized by limited numbers of leading or suggestive questions, a lack of motive for the child to make a false report, and a neutral stance by the interviewer (e.g., no coercion, acceptance of the child's statements without undue positive or negative emotion; see Chapter 6, "Friendly, Neutral Approach to Children," for more information). The interviewer should carefully document interviewing procedures, preferably via audio or video recording, so that other individuals can determine whether the interview was indeed neutral versus biased. (See Chapter 14, "Verbatim Documentation," for more details regarding recording options.)

7. BIASED INTERVIEWS CAN BE VERY PROBLEMATIC, PARTICULARLY WHEN THEY ARE NUMEROUS

Biased interviews are those in which the interviewer attempts to guide the child into making particular statements that confirm the interviewer's hypotheses about what happened to the child. Biased interviews typically will include one or more of the following components: asking numerous leading questions ("Your dad touched your privates, didn't he?"), making coercive statements ("You'll feel better once you tell," "I know something bad happened to you, don't be afraid to tell me"), making pejorative comments about the alleged perpetrator (e.g., "Bill is bad," "Bill does bad things," "Your friends told me what Bill did to them"), and/or providing support to the child only when the child discloses abuse. Research indicates that although children are typically accurate in neutral interviews, even in neutral interviews that contain one or two leading questions, some children will make false accusations when interviewed by a biased interviewer (see Ceci & Bruck, 1995, for a review). As the number of biasing factors increases and the number of biased interviews increases, the rates of false reports can rise dramatically. See Chapter 15, "Memory and Suggestibility," for a more complete review of the literature on interviewer bias.

8. CHILDREN'S STATEMENTS IN DIFFERENT INTERVIEWS ARE LIKELY TO BE INCONSISTENT

Inconsistency in a child's statements across interviews is frequently viewed as evidence of inaccuracy or fabrication. When adults are interviewed multiple times about the same event, some studies find that about 80% of the information is consistent from one report to another (McCloskey, Wible, & Cohen, 1988), whereas other studies have found lower rates of consistency for adults. Studies examining children's normal autobiographical recall show that consistency ranges from a high of about 60% for sixth-graders (Hudson & Fivush, 1987) to lows of 10% to 25% for preschoolers (Fivush & Hammond, 1990). Inconsistencies occur despite high levels of accuracy (90% in several studies). These effects have not been attributable to different interviewers (the effect is similar when children are interviewed by the same interviewer multiple times) or to contamination of the child's report during prior interviews (see Fivush, 1993, for a review).

> *Studies examining children's normal autobiographical recall show that inconsistencies occur despite high levels of accuracy.*

Some of the effect may have been attributable to different questions being posed in different interviews, because when children were asked precisely the same focused question, they did frequently provide the same answer. Fivush (1993) hypothesizes that the effect is largely attributable to developmental processes, whereby young children have not absorbed social norms regarding what to report about an event. She suggests that young children may require more support from the interviewer, in the form of specific questions and memory retrieval cues. (See Chapter 9, "Posing Appropriate Questions," for a discussion of the use of specific questions with preschoolers.)

❏   *Practice Tips*   ❏

1. Handling an extensive disclosure to the initial interviewer

It is important to acknowledge that some children will feel burdened by the secret and will "spill their guts" to the first person they are able to tell about the abuse. This person may be their parent, a teacher, a school counselor, a therapist, or a trusted caseworker. In these cases, the initial interviewer should respond just as in other cases. Specifically, the interviewer should support and reassure the child, and make every attempt to document the child's statements during the initial disclosure. Any questions should be open-ended rather than specific (see definitions of question types in Chapter 9, "Posing Appropriate Questions").

Under no circumstances should the initial interviewer try to stave off the disclosure until a center-based assessment can be arranged. It would be helpful for these initial interviewers to establish a link with the center assessment, letting children know that they appreciate the trust invested in them, and asking the children if they would be able to tell a special "talking person" who could help make sure the child was protected. This discussion should support the child's initial disclosure, while also explaining to the child why a second interview will be necessary. It should be clear from this conversation that a second interview does not mean the child was disbelieved after the first statement. What follows is an example of a good transition:

"I'm glad you told me about this problem. I want to make sure you're safe, and that grownups who can protect you know all about what happened. I think it would be helpful for you to have an appointment with a person who will want to know what you just told me, and who will ask some questions so (he or she) understands exactly what happened. Other kids I know have talked to this person, and the kids tell me (he or she) is very nice and easy to talk to. I will talk to your (nonoffending caretaker) about making an appointment for you."

In some cases, it may be helpful for this initial interviewer to be involved in the center-based assessment. It is important to note that although transitioning is helpful, the initial interviewer should not imply that the child must talk to the interviewer or that the child must tell exactly the same story to the interviewer. The general idea is that the children should understand that the interviewer will be there to help them and listen to whatever they have to say.

2. Center staff may need to instruct parents on handling child disclosures

It is helpful for parents to receive instruction from knowledgeable persons regarding how to respond if the child makes further statements. Ideally, the first professional to contact the parents (center intake personnel, police, child protection workers, or therapists) would instruct the parents to listen empathically to their child's statements and to offer emotional support, but to avoid further questioning. The parents should also be instructed to jot down the child's statements once they have supported the child. Center staff should work closely with other community professionals to ensure consistency in communicating with parents responding to child disclosures. It may also be helpful to include instructions to parents as part of the center's intake protocol.

3. Center interviewers may need to work with attorneys to ensure appropriate questioning

Increasingly, experts are emphasizing the need to hold accountable all persons who question a child regarding possible abuse, including the trial and pre-trial questioning conducted by attorneys. Assessment center interviewers can work with attorneys in a number of ways. For example, they can offer training sessions to local attorneys on child development, memory, and the importance of non-leading questions. Alternatively, the interviewer can work with the legal system to ensure that the videotaped interview(s) are the child's testimony, and attorneys for both sides are involved in certifying that all relevant information is contained in these interviews.

A similar approach is already being used in other countries (London Home Office and Department of Health, 1992).

❏ Cautionary Note

REPEATED INTERVIEWS SHOULD NEVER BE USED
TO "REHEARSE" A CHILD

Because each interview carries with it the potential for contamination of a child's report, multiple interviews should be utilized only when they are necessary to elicit a complete account. Even when the interviewer is neutral, recall errors have been noted to increase over multiple sessions, probably due to forgetting over time (Warren & Lane, 1995). This effect also may be attributable to the impact of repeating the same or similar questions. Repeated interviews with biased interviewers have produced numerous false allegations, fabricated elaborations on the child's narrative, and reports of non-events as actual experience (see Ceci & Bruck, 1995, for a review). Moreover, if a child appears rehearsed in court, he or she may be judged less credible as a witness (Flin, 1991).

6

Friendly, Neutral Approach to Children

❑ **Guideline**

The interviewer's demeanor with the child and the child's care-givers should be calm, warm, and welcoming. The interviewer must assume the role of a neutral information gatherer and should work to avoid having preconceptions regarding whether the child was or was not abused. This approach will strengthen the interview by putting the child and the parent at ease and encouraging trust in the interviewer.

❑ **Supporting Information**

1. FRIENDLY AND/OR NEUTRAL NONVERBAL BEHAVIORS ENHANCE INFORMATION QUALITY

It is noted by virtually every expert on child interviewing that rapport-building is an important initial phase that facilitates com-

42

munication and disclosure. When rapport is developed using open-ended questions that invite the child to speak freely, children who have experienced sexual abuse are more detailed in their disclosures (Lamb, Hershkowitz, Sternberg, Esplin, Hovav, Manor, & Yudilevitch, in press). Numerous studies of non-victims indicate that both children and adults are more accurate in the presence of a non-authoritative, supportive interviewer (Ceci, Ross, & Toglia, 1987b; Goodman, Bottoms, Schwartz-Kenney, & Rudy, 1991; Goodman, Sharma, Thomas, & Considine, 1995; Tobey & Goodman, 1992). Goodman and colleagues (1991) found that children speaking with a friendly, nurturant interviewer (who gave them cookies and juice at the beginning of the interview and was warm and praising throughout the interview) were more resistant to leading questions than children speaking with a more neutral interviewer (see Cautionary Note, later in this chapter). When 3- to 4-year-old children were interviewed by a neutral interviewer, their error rate doubled. The accuracy rate of 3- to 4-year-olds with a friendly interviewer was comparable to that of older children. Saywitz and colleagues (Saywitz, Geiselman, & Bornstein, 1992) compared positive, neutral, and condescending interview techniques and found that positive interviewers produced the greatest quantity of accurate details.

However, a concomitant increase in inaccurate details was also noted. The neutral interviewers produced fewer accurate details but also elicited the fewest number of inaccuracies.

A friendly, nurturant approach is recommended in the rapport-building phase.

In sum, studies of children who have not been victimized indicate that a friendly approach appears to be beneficial but to carry some risk of provoking inaccuracies. A neutral approach risks fewer inaccuracies but may be associated with missing some accurate information. It is important to note that a friendly approach is also likely to be associated with better psychological outcomes for the child, particularly a child who has experienced abuse. Consequently, a friendly, nurturant approach is recommended in the rapport-building phase, with the interviewer becoming more neutral as the interview progresses into the disclosure phase. If a child exhibits signs of distress, the interviewer can temporarily suspend questioning or switch, momentarily, to a less stressful topic. At these junctures, the interviewer can also suspend the neutral stance and adopt a nurturing tone of voice and/or body posture. Supportive comments and praise can be sprinkled throughout the interview, so long as they are not contingent on disclosures of abuse.

2. DESCRIPTION OF FRIENDLY AND NEUTRAL APPROACHES

Nonverbal communication is conveyed simultaneously through many channels. The key to a friendly approach is congruency. A smiling face needs to be matched with elevated vocal tones and body posture that is oriented toward the recipient. Eye gaze should be direct but nonthreatening. The interviewer should attempt to be on the same eye level as the recipient. For example, when greeting children, the interviewer can kneel down; when greeting parents, the interviewer can stand if they stand, or sit beside them if they remain seated. This sort of nonverbal behavior should be maintained during the greeting, as the child is introduced to the interview setting and as rapport-building begins.

Neutral nonverbal behavior is recommended during the questioning phase. The interviewer's vocal tones may be tailored to the child's needs (soft-spoken with soft-spoken children), and an interviewer should always feel free to communicate warmth and support through the voice. However, it is recommended that the interviewer be mindful regarding the timing of affirmative and negative head nods, writing the child's responses, and backchanneling statements ("uh-huh," "hmmm," "OK"), because these behaviors may imply an expected response (as in the case of affirmative head nods while the question is being posed) or may imply approval or disapproval of the child's answer to a question. The interviewer should either provide these responses noncontingently throughout the interview (e.g., during rapport-building and closure, as well as during disclosure) or should avoid these behaviors entirely. Verbal praise (e.g., "You're doing fine," "Smart girl," "You can count really high," "I know this is hard for you, but you're doing just fine"), if used, also should be noncontingent and should occur throughout the interview, irrespective of the quality of particular statements (see Cautionary Note, later in this chapter).

3. NEUTRAL RESPONSES TO CHILD DISCLOSURE

The interviewer should acknowledge a child's disclosure with neutral verbal and nonverbal responses such as backchanneling ("um hmm," head nods, "I see"), paraphrasing the child's statements ("You said that he took you into his bedroom"), and encouraging to continue running narratives ("What happened next?"; "Did anything else happen in your mother's bedroom?"; "How did the touching end?"). The interviewer should avoid affective reactions to the child's statements. Pleasure, as well as anger or disgust, is equally inappropriate. Indicators of pleasure communicate insensitivity to the impact of the abuse and the disclosure process on the child, and they suggest that the child is valued only for making disclosures. Indicators of anger and disgust at the perpetrator may inadvertently communicate similar feelings regarding the child's involvement in the abuse.

Anger and disgust also may bias the child's later responses, in that children may be more likely to make false accusations and acquiesce to leading suggestions. Lepore and Sesco (1994) interviewed children regarding games played with an experimenter. When interviewed in an incriminating versus a neutral mode, children were more likely to acquiesce to misleading questions about touching and kissing. The incriminating mode involved the interviewer placing value judgments on the child's report (e.g., "That was bad. What else did he do?"; "He shouldn't have done that"; "That was a bad touch"; "People who touch kids should be put in jail"). Similar outcomes have occurred in other studies, in which children were told before meeting a person that the person was clumsy (Leichtman & Ceci, 1995) and/or were told after observing a neutral event that the "perpetrator's" behavior during the event was bad (Clarke-Stewart, Thompson, & Lepore, 1989).

Though these studies did not involve children who had experienced abuse, it seems clear that a similar outcome could occur with such a child, particularly when the child already is angry or feels vindictive toward the perpetrator. Moreover, it is important not to lose sight of the forensic relevance of studies with nonabused children. Some children in forensic contexts have not been abused, and it is relevant to know if nonabused children can be led into making false accusations using the same techniques that are used to support disclosure from children who have experienced abuse. Interviewer bias is consistently associated with high rates of false reports among non-victims.

4. THE POTENTIAL NEGATIVE IMPACT OF BIASES

Interviewer bias can take several forms. Overly positive or negative reactions to the child's disclosure are one indicator of interviewer bias, as noted earlier. When an interviewer enters the conversation with a child, carrying preconceived notions (e.g., "I dislike interviews with hyperactive boys"; "This is just a custody battle, this child wasn't really abused"; "This perpetrator is a jerk, I hope he gets punished"; "You shouldn't leave your children with teenage boys, they can't control their impulses"), the interviewer's questions, responses to the child's statements, and nonverbal behavior may evidence a bias (Faller, 1996a). Biased nonverbal behavior can include suggestive head nods (slight negative head nods while asking if a child was touched in the privates), tense vocal tones, contingent writing (only when abuse is disclosed), leaning forward or away as a child discloses, and so forth. Biased verbal behavior includes phrasing questions so that compliance with the interviewer's bias is encouraged (e.g., asking leading or coercive questions). These biases are very difficult to monitor and may alter behavior without conscious control.

> *When an interviewer carries preconceived notions into the interview, his or her questions, responses, and nonverbal behavior may evidence a bias.*

A long tradition of psychological research indicates that biases affect the outcomes of social interactions in numerous settings, such that when there is a power differential between conversants, the less powerful individual is likely to attempt to please the more powerful individual through statements and behavior (Ney, 1995; Rosenthal,

1985; Rosenthal & Rubin, 1978). Child interviewing studies indicate that interviewer biases provoke erroneous child reports and lead to inaccurate descriptions of the child's report by the interviewer (Ceci, Leichtman, & White, 1995; Dent, 1982; Goodman, Sharma, Thomas, & Considine, 1995). Dent (1982) noted that interviewers who formed a preconceived notion of what happened during a staged event elicited the highest proportion of incorrect information. The interviewers in these studies questioned in a suggestive manner regarding the preconceived interpretation, and they tended to ignore information inconsistent with their biases. Similarly, other researchers have primed interviewers with accurate versus inaccurate information, and then asked them to elicit event reports from children (cf., Ceci, Leichtman, & White, 1995). Interviewers with inaccurate information asked misleading questions, elicited high rates of inaccurate information and false reports, and ignored inconsistent information in describing the child's report.

Goodman and colleagues (1995) noted that children tended to "shut down" with biased interviewers, in that they reported less information and made statements such as "That's all we did," which may have been attempts to deflect biased questioning. These children also added more fantasy material and inaccurate statements into their descriptions than did children talking with unbiased interviewers.

It is therefore critically important that interviewers be able to self-monitor regarding biases and that they develop coping skills to counteract biases. Live and/or videotaped supervision can be very useful in this regard.

5. A NOTE ON "TESTING AN ALTERNATIVE HYPOTHESIS"

Social scientists have developed several procedures to guard against interviewer bias during research studies, including having the interviewer remain uninformed (i.e., "blind") regarding the major hypotheses of the study and testing a specific alternative hypothesis in the same study as the primary hypothesis. Ceci & Bruck (1995) argue that forensic interviewers should utilize these same procedures to guard against bias during their interviews.

Providing the interviewer with minimal information regarding the allegation may be a legitimate approach to guarding against interviewer bias (see Chapter 7, "Gathering and Documenting Background Information," for more details). Before being widely adopted, the effectiveness of the "history-free" approach to interviewing needs to be carefully examined in both clinical and research contexts, because the forensic interviewer can never be completely blind (e.g., the child is seeing the interviewer due to a concern regarding abuse). Some interviewers are currently exploring the utility of history-free interviewing. This clinical exploration must be supplemented by experimental studies that are forensically relevant (e.g., comparing children's statements with interviewers given minimal incorrect information, versus interviewers given information that is incorrect along with information that there may be reason to be suspicious of the information provided).

The authors of these guidelines are concerned about potential misapplications of the recommendation to test a specific alternative hypothesis during a forensic interview. We agree with Ceci and Bruck regarding the need to avoid "confirmatory bias" or the dogged pursuit of the hypothesis that the child was sexually abused. In these guidelines, the interviewer is repeatedly encouraged to remain open to the possibility that no abuse occurred (labeled the "null hypothesis" by researchers). For example, the interviewer is encouraged (a) to ask the parent and the child about other sources of sexual knowledge, (b) to inquire about the quality of previous interviews with the child, (c) to refrain from asking leading or coercive questions, and (d) to ask children about information sources and coaching, when the source of the child's report is at issue. Moreover, the interviewer is admonished to (e) institute self and peer monitoring via videotape review, and (f) formulate questions to examine concerns regarding a child's credibility. The responses of the legal system to videotapes of biased interviews also constitute a formidable quality control mechanism. Not all of these procedures will be necessary in every interview, but the greater the concern regarding the child's credibility, the more these options should be utilized.

Although we agree with the need to monitor biases and reduce their influence on child interviews, we depart from Ceci and Bruck at the point when the interviewer is encouraged to ask leading questions about a specific alternative hypothesis. Whereas Ceci and Bruck recommend questions we feel are appropriate in some circumstances ("Did that really happen?," and "Did someone tell you this happened, or did you see it happen?"), they also suggest saying to a child, "You're kidding me, aren't you," and "Who else besides your

> *Asking leading questions regarding a specific alternative hypothesis is not a viable solution to interviewer bias.*

teacher touched your private parts? Did mommy touch them, too?" We feel strongly that **asking leading questions regarding a specific alternative hypothesis is NOT a viable solution to the problem of interviewer bias.** If the child acquiesces to leading questions about the alternative hypothesis, two possibilities exist: (1) The child told the truth about the abuse (possibly in response to a neutral and non-leading set of questions), but acquiesced to the leading questions about the alternative hypothesis; or (2) the child made a false report of abuse and acquiesced to leading questions about the alternative hypothesis. It may not be possible to discriminate between these two possibilities. The approach recommended by Ceci and Bruck risks unneccessarily discrediting the reports of children who have actually experienced abuse. See Chapter 15, "Memory and Suggestibility," and Chapter 16, "Errors in Child Reports," for more suggestions for handling concerns about child credibility.

❑   *Practice Tips*   ❑

1. The interviewer should welcome the child and the caregivers warmly

This gesture creates goodwill with the parent/guardian. At the same time, it begins the transfer of temporary parental authority to the interviewer. Children (particularly young ones) may model their parents' responses to the interviewer and/or may be looking for signs of parental approval before electing to "open up."

2. **Interviewers should have a positive expectation that they will like the child and will be liked by the child**

Mental imaging of one's nonverbal greeting can make the expectation a reality. If an interviewer finds a particular child difficult, he or she should actively look for qualities of the child that are endearing or admirable. For example, a "plucky" child may have learned to survive in a hostile world at the expense of reliance upon adults.

3. **Live and/or videotaped supervision and viewing of one's own videotapes are a useful safeguard against biased behavior**

Many individuals exhibit habitual behavior patterns such as head nods and backchanneling that are useful feedback mechanisms when they occur in the context of everyday conversation. However, critics of any given interview may legitimately claim bias if an interviewer's nonverbal support and encouragement appears contingent upon particular disclosures. Viewing and having others review live and/or recorded interviews with these issues in mind can be invaluable in identifying and correcting what are often unconscious, overlearned responses.

4. **Formulating questions to test a bias can be a helpful strategy**

If an interviewer is concerned about a particular child's presentation or the context of his or her disclosures, it is helpful to formulate questions to examine these biases. Ideally, these questions would be held until the end of the interview, and if the concern remained, the questions could be posed. For example, if there is a suspicion that a child has been coached, the interviewer can ask the child if there were conversations about abuse with potentially biased caretakers (e.g., "Did ___ talk to you about the touching? What did they say?"). If the interviewer is worried that a child is creating allegations for vengeance motives, questions can be posed about feelings toward the alleged perpetrator before and after the touching happened and/or sources of different pieces of information (e.g., "How do you feel about ___ now? How did you feel when you first met him? What changed your mind? What do you want to happen to ___? What does *potentially biased person* want?"). See Chapter 16, "Errors in Children's Reports," for more suggestions on formulating questions to examine concerns about child credibility.

Formulating the questions prior to entering the interview situation can help the interviewer to temporarily put these issues aside and focus on the child's unchallenged statements, at least initially.

Some interviewer biases can be addressed during the process of gathering social history. If interviewers are worried about working with a child they are prone to dislike, they can ask the parents to describe the child's positive qualities. The interviewer may also want to ask about alternative sources of sexual knowledge, other risk factors that may account for the child's behavior, and the caretaker's prior conversations with the child about the allegation during the social history. See Chapter 7, "Gathering and Documenting Background Information," for more suggestions.

5. Self "pep talks" are a useful guard against bias

If interviewers perceive a bias with a particular child, it can be helpful for them to remind themselves that it is not their job to determine the statement's ultimate validity. The interviewer's primary function is to elicit the statement from the child, using a nonbiased questioning format and interview context. The interviewer can be either helpful by supporting the child and aiding recall or hurtful by providing contaminating information. Ultimate determinations regarding the

child's credibility should be made after the interview is complete.

❏ **Cautionary Note**

IT IS CRITICAL TO USE PRAISE AND
TREATS NONCONTINGENTLY

It is very damaging to the integrity of the interview for the
interviewer to praise the child only for disclosure or to offer the child
snacks and treats only if he or she discloses (e.g., "As soon as you
tell me what happened, we'll get a teddy bear out of my special
cabinet"; "We can't get a snack until I know what happened with
your daddy"). Making such gestures contingent on the child's disclosure changes the meaning of the behavior from being an indicator
of generosity and a desire to nurture the child to one of coercion and
bribing. If snacks are offered, it is recommended that they be offered
to every child prior to the interview. When treats (teddy bears,
stickers, toys) are used, they should be offered to all children,
regardless of whether they disclose. There are advantages to offering the treat prior to the evaluation, in that it is clear that there is no
contingency between disclosure and treats, and if the treat is a
stuffed animal, the child can use it for comfort throughout the
evaluation. It should be made clear to the child that the treat is given
to all children.

For some people, noncontingent praise is difficult to master (e.g.,
saying "You're doing fine" throughout the interview, even if the
child is making nonsensical disclosures, is suggestible, or is refusing
to disclose). These individuals should praise only during initial
phases, prior to the child's disclosure, and at the end of the interview
(e.g., "Thank you for talking with me today").

7

Gathering and Documenting Background Information

☐ **Guideline**

The type of information gathered depends upon the purposes of the evaluation. Information likely to be important for any child interviewer includes descriptions of prior interviews, sources of sexual knowledge, and current experience with nonabusive genital touch (e.g., bathing, toileting, and genital exams at the doctor's office).

☐ **Supporting Information**

1. SOME PROFESSIONALS BELIEVE THE INTERVIEWER
   IS MOST NEUTRAL WITHOUT INFORMATION ABOUT
   THE SPECIFIC ALLEGATIONS

Because biases regarding the perpetrator or the child's prior statements can color behavior, some researchers and clinicians advocate for a "history-free" conversation with the child (Cantlon, Payne, & Erbaugh, 1996; Sorenson, Bottoms, & Perona, 1997). The terms *history-free* and *allegation-blind* are used when the interviewer speaks to the child without knowledge of the specifics of the allegation or the child's family background. Of course, interviewers typically will know that there is a concern of abuse; therefore, interviews are rarely completely blind. In a series of studies comparing children's disclosure rates using allegation-blind versus allegation-informed interviews, 94% of children ages 6 and older disclosed when the interviewer was not informed of the allegation. Of children ages 4 to 6, 18% disclosed only after the interviewer was able to focus questioning on the basis of the available history (Cantlon et al., 1996; Cantlon, personal communication). Of note, even advocates of this approach advise against allegation blind interviews with children under the age of 4. This approach is distinctly advantageous in legal settings, because it reduces concerns regarding interviewer bias.

Although information about the allegation and family background may be biasing, it may also inform questioning. There has been little research directly comparing levels of interviewer bias and the quality of the child's statements with allegation-blind and allegation-informed approaches; thus, both approaches remain valid choices for child abuse evaluation centers.

Information about prior interviews, sources of sexual knowledge, and current experience with nonabusive genital touch are critical to evaluation.

For those who choose to interview with a knowledge of background information and allegation specifics, videotaping permits evaluation of both the presence of bias and the effect on the child's statements. Videotaping thus provides a safeguard, in the sense that biased interviews will be exposed. See Chapter 14, "Verbatim Documentation," for more information.

Information about prior interviews, sources of sexual knowledge, and current experience with nonabusive genital touch are critical to evaluating the child's statements. If the interviewer chooses not to gather this information prior to the interview, then either the investigator (law enforcement or child protection) should gather this information or the interviewer can gather the information after completion of the interview.

Some centers combine the approaches, with a history-free initial interview, a break while the interviewer gathers information, and a second interview following history-gathering (Cantlon et al., 1996). Cantlon (personal communication, 1997) notes that among older children, most disclose during the history-free section of the interview, and the history does not significantly increase disclosure rates. Among children ages 4 to 6, focused questioning after gathering history significantly increases disclosure rates. Therefore, a completely history-free interview is not advisable for children under the age of 6.

2. IN SOME CASES, THE HISTORY-FREE APPROACH MAY NOT BE JUSTIFIABLE

It is important to note that the history-free interview may be a less viable approach with disabled clients, children involved in custody evaluations, and very young children. Information about disabilities allows the interviewer to accommodate the child's needs, in order to effectively question the child and to minimize stress to the child. It may be difficult to gather information about the child's disability, without the caretaker "spilling" other information about the allegation. When coaching or parental bias is a concern in a custody battle, the interviewer may need to know the sources of concern in order to formulate questions to test whether adult biases have impacted the child's statements. Finally, memory limitations with younger children sometimes mean that only particular cues will elicit an accurate account. Reviewing children's prior disclosures, daily routines, and their names for salient caretakers and family members can provide invaluable assistance to the interviewer in cueing child memory. For those invested in a history-free interview, the combined approach may work best with custody evaluations and young children. Specifically, a history-free interview would be conducted first, a break would be taken while the child checks in with caretakers and the interviewer gathers history to gauge further questioning, and a decision would be made regarding whether to have a second interview session with the child. See the Guidelines for Chapter 15, "Memory and Suggestibility," Chapter 18, "Interviewing the Special Needs Child," and Chapter 19, "Coping With Custody and Visitation Disputes," for more details.

3. DESCRIPTIONS OF PRIOR INTERVIEWS GUIDE
QUESTIONING IN THE CURRENT INTERVIEW

Interview here is broadly defined to encompass conversations with parents, teachers, law enforcement, child protection workers, or any other adult who questioned the child. Descriptions of prior interviews permit evaluation of sources of contamination such as coaching, leading questions, or badgering with multiple interviews by multiple individuals. **Knowledge of potential contamination** guides the interviewer in framing questions pertaining to the child's sources of information (e.g., "How did you know Ben touched Susie?"). See Chapter 16, "Errors in Children's Reports," and Chapter 17, "The Nondisclosing Child," for more examples. **Knowledge of tools** (anatomical dolls, drawings) used during the prior interviews allows the interviewer to make an informed judgment regarding whether reusing the same tool might be comforting to a child, or whether repeating use of the tool might be leading or suggestive. Summaries of prior interviews also provide information regarding spontaneity of the original disclosure, and with young children, possible cues for triggering the child's memory (e.g., using the word *poking* versus *touching* in questions). Also, if a child has been thoroughly and competently interviewed by law enforcement or child protection personnel, the merits of a second interview should be carefully considered.

4. ASKING ABOUT SEXUAL KNOWLEDGE AND GENITAL
TOUCH PERMITS EXPLORATION OF ALTERNATIVE
EXPLANATIONS FOR THE CHILD'S DISCLOSURE

At times, a child may make an alarming statement based on sexual knowledge and experience rather than on sexual abuse. For example, "Daddy poked my pee pee" may refer to an accident during bathing or toileting; "You have sex by going up and down on each other" may stem from viewing adult programming; and one child inserting something into another's vagina may result from witnessing maternal tampon insertion. In evaluating young children, information regarding bathing, toileting, and bedtime rituals is particularly important, because these are times of both increased risk of misunderstanding and increased access for perpetrators. Exposure to pornography, adult television programming, walking in on parental sexual activity, nudity in the home, and prior genital exams can also provoke actions or statements concerning sexual abuse. The interviewer should question the parents about these issues.

5. ASKING ABOUT NONOFFENDING ADULTS' REACTIONS TO THE DISCLOSURE IS INFORMATIVE

It is particularly instructive to ask about reactions to the initial disclosure and about familial reactions that may have occurred in the child's presence. Some caretakers are shocked by the child's disclosure and have an initial reaction of disbelief, or anger at the perpetrator, which inadvertently discourages the child from making further disclosures. At times, family members try to explore alternative hypotheses with the child, express their disbelief in front of the child, or even attempt to force the child to recant. Asking both parents and child about the parents' and other people's reactions to the disclosure can provide important information regarding the need for child protection services or the need for family intervention. This information can also explain recantation and can be helpful in allowing the interviewer to question the child regarding reasons for recantation. (See Chapter 17, "The Nondisclosing Child," for detailed approaches to handling this situation in the interview.)

6. DEMOGRAPHIC INFORMATION PERMITS AN INDIVIDUALIZED APPROACH TO QUESTIONING

Information about the child's age, grade in school, learning disabilities, and developmental delays allows the interviewer to gauge questions to the child's level of comprehension. For example, a child with auditory perception problems can be engaged with drawings or dolls for improved communication between child and interviewer.

Information about names of family members, current and past caretakers, people who have lived in the family's home, and parents' current and past partners is helpful, particularly with a young child, who may name a person but be unable to articulate the person's role in his or her life or who may name a person with poor articulation. It is especially helpful to know if the child has nicknames or pet names for any of these individuals (e.g., Na Na or Maw Maw for grandma). Name information can also be helpful in developing a neutral list of individuals for asking "likes/dislikes" questions.

Use of information not given by the child reinforces the child's idea of adult omniscience.

Of course, the interviewer should try to elicit name information from the child and should generally only use information obtained from the child during the interview. Use of information not given by the child reinforces the child's idea of adult omniscience and may interfere with the child's willingness to supply details later in the interview. As a last resort, if the child is not able to name important people, the interviewer may want to inform the child that the interviewer spoke to the child's mother and the mother talked about some important people. The interviewer can name these people and ask the child to tell the interviewer about these people (e.g., "Tell me about Uncle Bob"; or "What do you like to do with Uncle Bob? Does Uncle Bob do things you don't like?").

7. ADDITIONAL HISTORY IS NECESSARY IF THE EVALUATOR INTENDS TO DEFINE TREATMENT GOALS

For some centers, particularly those located in medical settings, the purpose of the evaluation includes defining treatment goals for the child and family. In these cases, assessment of risk factor exposure (parental divorce, approaches to discipline, especially physical discipline, domestic violence, drug and alcohol abuse, and criminal activity), family history of mental illness, and familial incidence of child physical abuse, sexual abuse, and neglect will provide important information regarding potential family treatment foci. This information is also critical in determining the need for child protection services. Moreover, the evaluator will want to know about the child's behavioral and emotional functioning, as well as recent family stressors, in order to better gauge the child's need for various treatment modalities (individual versus group) and treatment intensity (outpatient, inpatient). A description of when problems started and the frequency of problem behaviors is useful in exploring possible linkages with the abusive activity. It should be noted that parents may need help in understanding that there are no definitive behavioral indicators of child abuse but that child behavior changes may be associated with family stress, including child abuse. In discussing behavior problems with the parents, the interviewer should be prepared to clarify this point if necessary.

In centers utilizing this model, the child abuse evaluation represents an opportunity for the family to receive a comprehensive evaluation by medical and mental health experts. The evaluation provides suggestions to improve child and family functioning in areas that may have been previously unidentified. Of course, this extended model is more expensive, and some families may feel that the additional questions are intrusive.

> *It is important to provide follow-up to families to permit access to recommended treatment resources.*

When centers utilize the extended model, it is important that they provide follow-up to families to permit access to recommended treatment resources. Follow-up can occur through onsite treatment, involvement of child protection agencies, or specific mental health referrals (provided either by the interviewer verbally or in written form, by volunteer court appointed special advocates or onsite mental health consultants).

❏ *Practice Tips* ❏

1. Social history forms are big time-savers

Social history forms asking all but the most sensitive questions can be completed in advance by parents or other caretakers and only briefly reviewed by the interviewer prior to evaluating the child. See Appendix B for an example of a social history form.

2. Sensitive questions should be asked in person

The interviewer may choose to ask the parents about their own drug and alcohol use, domestic violence in the current marriage, parental criminal or mental health history, or the parents' personal history of childhood victimization (physical and sexual abuse). These questions are best asked in person because the parents are more likely to provide a valid answer if they have met the interviewer and feel some ability to trust the interviewer. It is also helpful for the interviewer to be present to handle any adverse reactions parents have to the questions (sadness, anger).

3. Standardized behavior problem checklists are useful summaries of child functioning

Standardized behavior problem checklists are typically quite thorough in evaluating domains of child functioning (e.g., anxiety, depression, defiance) and permit more accurate comparisons of the child's functioning relative to "normal" children. The checklist can be completed in advance by the child's caretaker and can be computer- or hand-scored relatively quickly prior to, or during, the child's evaluation. Checklist scores can be very helpful in evaluating the child's treatment needs. They can also be helpful in communicating with parents regarding the level of difficulty the child is experiencing. These checklists are also frequently used by treatment providers and so are helpful in communicating about child adjustment problems.

PART II

Basic Interviewing Skills

8

Setting the Stage

❏ Guideline

Young children possess limited knowledge of the task demands in the forensic interview, including the kinds of information and the level of detail they are expected to report. Interviewers must be prepared to orient the child to expected roles for child and interviewer, rules of communication, and the reasons for the interview.

❏ Supporting Information

1. CHILDREN MAY HAVE MANY QUESTIONS AND MISUNDERSTANDINGS ABOUT THE INTERVIEW

Some children may be uncertain whether it is acceptable to discuss family secrets or topics that are taboo in our society (sex, family violence). Even when children understand that the purpose of the interview is to discuss these topics, their ability to share sensitive information will depend upon rapport with the interviewer (see Chapter 6, "Friendly, Neutral Approach to Children," for more details). Young children are unlikely to comprehend differences between the interview and normal conversations with parents and teachers (Brennan & Brennan, 1988). For example, in the interview there is no right or wrong answer, the adult is less knowledgeable than the child about relevant events, guessing is not a good idea, the child will be doing most of the talking, and the child can contradict the adult when the adult is wrong (Ceci & Bruck, 1993). See Sections 8 through 12 in this chapter for suggestions regarding how to clarify these issues with a child prior to questioning about possible abuse.

2. ASSESSMENT OF LANGUAGE USAGE AND CONCEPTUAL UNDERSTANDING IS HELPFUL

In order to make questions comprehensible to the child, the interviewer must listen to the child's sentences and match language to the child's language as much as possible (Walker, 1994). The interviewer will likely be using concepts such as inside/outside, underneath/on top of, first/last, and the number of times an event occurred. Finally, the interviewer may want to examine the child's ability to understand the obligation to be truthful and make distinctions between fact and fantasy (Yuille et al., 1993). Interviewers may choose to examine the child's understanding of these concepts ahead of time, in order to phrase questions differently or avoid certain issues entirely. Interviewers may also choose to assess conceptual understanding only if the particular issue arises during the child's disclosure. For a complete discussion of risks and benefits of this type of questioning, please see Sections 11 and 12 in this chapter.

> *The interviewer may want to examine the child's ability to understand the obligation to be truthful.*

3. SUMMARY OF "STAGE-SETTING" GOALS

The overall goal of the initial section is to establish a unique relationship with the child that involves questions and answers in a context the child experiences as supportive enough and neutral enough to permit disclosure of sensitive information. The interviewer must define the unique relationship, must exude a child-friendly attitude, and may need to assess the skills the child brings to the situation. The following task list summarizes the stage to be set. Each skill will be discussed in upcoming sections.

- Defining the interviewer's role
- Building rapport
- Telling the child what to expect, giving the child control
- Informed consent about observers and/or taping
- Developmental assessment
- Defining the child's role

4. DEFINING THE INTERVIEWER'S ROLE:
SOLICITING THE CAREGIVER'S HELP

At some point prior to meeting with the child, it is helpful to provide instruction to the child's caretaker regarding the purposes of the interview. Whenever possible at the time of scheduling, intake personnel should inform the parent about recording procedures, center rules regarding parental presence during the interview, and access to recordings of the procedure. At this time, it is also helpful to guide the parent in describing the evaluation to the child. The intake person can provide suggestions, such as "There will be a special talking person asking you questions about the touching you told me about," or in a medical center, "Your whole body will be checked, even your private parts. The doctor and her helper will also talk to you to help make sure you're safe."

At the time of the appointment, the interviewer should ask the caregiver, away from the child, what the child was told about the evaluation. It is also helpful at this point to ask the caregivers if they had any expectations about the gender of the evaluator(s) and to remind them about center policies regarding caregiver presence during the interview and caregiver access to recorded materials. It is helpful to have caregivers sign a consent form indicating their willingness to comply with these policies.

Once the interviewer's role is understood, the caregiver can be encouraged to sanction the interview in the child's presence. The interviewer can ask the adult to say something like "(Name of interviewer) is good at talking to kids and listening to kids." Alternatively, the interviewer can, in the caregiver's presence, ask permission to talk to the child, for example, "It's time for Suzy and me to talk. I want to know if it's alright if Suzy talks about anything she wants."

5. INITIAL GOALS ARE BEST ACCOMPLISHED WHOLISTICALLY, RATHER THAN SEQUENTIALLY

Some interviewers view each of the stage-setting tasks as separate parts of the beginning phase. These tasks can also be accomplished artfully by centering the child's attention on a single broad activity (a colorful ABC chart, body part naming) and embedding assessment in the broader activity. The wholistic approach may be preferable for holding a young child's attention and in conserving the time taken to accomplish numerous forensic tasks. See the "Practice Tips" section later in this chapter for examples of wholistic assessment strategies.

6. RAPPORT DEVELOPMENT IS NOT A FREE-STANDING TASK

Rapport refers to development of a positive relationship between the interviewer and child. Rapport development is associated with greater accuracy in event reports (Ceci, Ross, & Toglia, 1987a; Dent, 1982; Goodman, Bottoms, Schwartz-Kenney, & Rudy, 1991; Lamb, Hershkowitz, et al., in press). The interviewer's questioning style, nonverbal behavior, attentiveness to the child, and ability to engage the child in developmentally appropriate tasks will be the primary determinants of rapport development. Developmental assessment, if conducted in a lighthearted manner, sprinkled with praise and personal comments, **is** rapport development. Rapport will be developed if the interviewer is kind to the child (providing snacks, friendly voice), gets along with the child's parents, praises the child for accomplishing tasks in the developmental assessment, asks open-ended questions about the child and listens attentively to the child's responses without interrupting, engages the child in an age-appropriate task (e.g., an ABC chart or body part naming with a preschooler, discussions of favorite activities or pets with older children), and shares small amounts of personal information with the child ("We almost had the same birthday! My birthday is the day after yours"; "I once had a pet rat, too. I had a lot of fun with my rat, how about you?").

7. AN OPEN-ENDED QUESTIONING APPROACH SHOULD BE USED DURING STAGE-SETTING

As the interviewer begins conversing with the child, the types of questions used help define the interaction. A primary goal of the initial section is to communicate to the child that the interviewer is interested in the child's statements and would like the child to comment at length in response to questions. Open-ended questions (e.g., "How are you doing today?"; "What do you do to have fun?"; "Who lives with you?") are best for eliciting detailed responses in this phase as in other phases of the interview (see Chapter 9, "Posing Appropriate Questions," for examples and definitions of different types of questions). A recent study of interviews with sexually abused children examined differential effects of using open versus closed questions during the initial phase of the interview (Lamb, Hershkowitz, et al., in press). Following the initial phase, all children were asked an open question to transition into the abuse-questioning phase (e.g., "I understand that something may have happened to you. Tell me about that"). Responses to the transition question were 2.5 times as long and were replete with forensically relevant details among the children whose initial phase was conducted with open-ended questions. Thus, the type of questions posed during the initial phase of the interview influenced the length and relevance of responses during the abuse-focused portion of the interview.

8. DEFINING THE INTERVIEWER'S ROLE: TALKING WITH THE CHILD

Before the interviewer explains roles, it is helpful to ask children who they think the interviewer is and what they expect to happen during the interview. This permits the interviewer to clarify misconceptions. For example, young children may think you are a doctor and will give them a shot. Other children may think you are a police officer or a lawyer.

> *It is helpful to tell the child that your job is to talk to kids, and that you have talked with many kids in the past.*

It is helpful to tell the child that your job is to talk with kids and that you have talked with many kids in the past. You can tell the child that you will ask some questions and will listen carefully to the answers. You can also tell the child that you talk to kids about things that bother them or problems they are having.

9. TELLING THE CHILD WHAT TO EXPECT

At around the same time the interviewer is defining roles, it is helpful to let the child know what to expect. Children often want to know how long you will be talking ("a little while" for a young child, or "about an hour" for a child 7 or older). In addition, a simple explanation of the sorts of issues that will be covered is helpful to many children (e.g., "I talk to kids about their families, about things they like, and about things that bother or worry them," or "First we will be getting to know each other a bit, then we'll talk about why you're here today, then you can ask some questions and we'll go see your mom").

10. GIVING THE CHILD A SENSE OF CONTROL

It is important to meet the child's unspoken need to feel control. Giving the child choices about where to sit, what activities to use (charts, drawings, dolls, his or her own body), how loudly to talk, and so forth, helps the child feel more in control of a strange situation. It may also be helpful to point out that the interview room has no locks and that the child can leave if he or she wishes. With a young child, confirm that the caretaker is nearby and available, if the child needs to check in. Providing the child with drinks and snacks and pointing out the location of bathrooms can help the child feel in control of biological needs.

11. INFORMED CONSENT ABOUT OBSERVERS AND TAPING

Especially with older children, their ability to trust the interviewer may be fragile. It is important that the child understand that observers are present and that the interview is being recorded. Some interviewers also provide these explanations to younger children. Decisions about how much information to give the child about observers (e.g., identified by name, by role, or only a general reference such as "There are people in the room next door and they can hear us and see us") and taping (e.g., a general reference versus a full description of the reasons for taping and possible tape distribution) will vary on a case-by-case basis, depending on the comfort levels of both the child and the interviewer and on indications from the child regarding how much information he or she would like to have. What follows are some examples of informed consent:

"I want to tell you a little bit about my special talking room. See that mirror. Over there is a room with people in it. Those people can hear us and see us. There's also a machine that takes down our words and makes pictures of us while we talk."

"See that mirror. It's called a one-way mirror. What that means is it's a mirror on one side, our side, but it's a window on the other side. Other people who help children can sit over there and watch while we talk. Right now, _____ (detective) and _____ (caseworker) are over there, and they can hear us and see us. There's also a camera making a tape of us while we talk. That tape helps me remember what we talk about."

The interviewer should be prepared to reassure children if they are worried their parents or the perpetrator might see the tape. The reassurances must be realistic, however. For example, "We only let people whose job is to protect children sit over there. We don't even let your parents watch while we make the tape." The interviewer should not promise the child that the child's parents or the perpetrator will never know the contents of the tape. The interviewer can promise that the tape will not end up on the news or in a video store.

Please note that in most cases, items 7 through 10 collectively take no more than 5 to 10 minutes.

12. DEVELOPMENTAL ASSESSMENT

Activities included in the developmental assessment vary tremendously with the child's age. With a young child, this portion of the interview may be fairly extensive (5 to 10 minutes), whereas with a teenager, this section may be completely unneccesary (see the "Practice Tips" section in this chapter for examples of approaches to developmental assessment).

With children up to 6 years old, the interviewer may want to test color labeling, counting, number relational concepts (more/less, first/last), time comprehension (ability to say current age, age at past events, night/day, seasons), forensic locator concepts (inside/outside, under/on top of), the ability to distinguish fantasy from reality and truth from lie, basic autobiographical information (who is in the family, the name of their babysitter[s], child's own name and age), and body part labels. It is important to note that there are potential risks as well as benefits to conducting an extensive developmental assessment of this nature with young children. Although this assessment may contribute to perceptions of child credibility and is reassuring regarding language comprehension, an extensive assessment may conflict with the overall goals of the interview. Specifically, many of the questions in this section have right versus wrong answers defined by the interviewer, and the assessment does not encourage the child to provide detailed narratives. As such, the developmental assessment may undermine the interviewer's attempt to distinguish this conversation from conversations with parents and teachers and may set up the child to provide brief answers (Lamb, Hershkowitz, et al., in press). If the

> *There are potential risks as well as benefits to conducting extensive developmental assessment with young children.*

assessment is too extensive, the child might be exhausted before abuse-focused questioning begins.

The interviewer may want to assess conceptual understanding as these issues arise during the interview. In fact, it may even be helpful to assess these issues at the end of the interview. The problems regarding time allocation and provision of detailed narratives can also be partially ameliorated by having the interviewer restrict specific questioning about forensic concepts (truth/lie, number relations, inside/outside, etc.) to no more than a couple of minutes, and to follow this questioning with open-ended questioning to elicit autobiographical narratives.

With school-age children, the interviewer can assume knowledge of many concepts, and can focus on ability to relate event timing (using seasons, proximity to holidays) and ability to provide autobiographical narratives. The interviewer can ask children to tell about a salient event, and conduct a short practice interview regarding the event, including encouraging them to tell who was there, what happened, where they were (with peripheral detail), and when it occurred. The interviewer can praise children when they spontaneously do well, can encourage them to provide missing information, and can notify them that similar narratives will be desired regarding other events to be discussed. In research with both abused and non-abused children, practice interviews containing open-ended questions and descriptions of ground rules have increased the amount of accurate information produced by children aged 7 and older (Geiselman, Saywitz, & Bornstein, 1993; Lamb, Hershkowitz, et al., in press; Yuille et al., 1993).

13. DEFINING THE CHILD'S ROLE

The interviewer will need to alert the child to differences between this conversation and other conversations between children and adults (Yuille et al., 1993). Some researchers refer to this process as establishing the "ground rules" for the interview (McGough & Warren, 1994; Saywitz & Snyder, 1993). Research studies indicate that explication of the ground rules reduces children's suggestibility and enhances resistance to misleading questions (Toglia, Ross, Ceci, & Hembrooke, 1992; Warren, Hulse-Trotter, & Tubbs, 1991).

It is helpful to convey that the interviewer's primary interest is the child's welfare and to **underscore the interviewer's impartiality** regarding the child's statements. For example, the interviewer can say, "I just want to find out how things are going with you by asking a few questions, and listening. Anything you say in here is OK, and you won't get in trouble."

The interviewer may want to emphasize the **importance of telling the truth.** With children over the age of 10, it may be helpful to say something like, "It's important that we are both careful what we say in here. I'm going to make sure I tell you the truth, and I want to know if you will tell me the truth. Will you do that?" With preschool and young school-age children, the interviewer may want to establish conceptual understanding before asking the child to tell the truth and may need to be prepared to discuss this issue in more than one way, depending on the child's comprehension of real/pretend and truth/lie, for example, "Today we are only going to talk about things that really happened," versus "We both need to tell the truth today, OK?" (see "Practice Tips" later in this chapter, for more suggestions). In the legal system, it is important to establish that a witness can appreciate the obligation to be truthful and that the witness agrees to provide truthful statements during testimony. To the extent that children's videotaped statements may supplement or substitute for their testimony in courtroom settings, it may be necessary for the interviewer to cover these issues. However, it is important to note that in several research studies, children admonished to tell the truth become overly cautious and overuse "I don't know" in responding to questions, when compared to children who were not given the warning about truthfulness (Saywitz, Moan, & Lamphear, 1991, as cited in Saywitz & Snyder, 1993). Finally, when children believe something that has been suggested to them but that is untrue, they are not lying even though they are making a false report. Consequently, establishing their ability to distinguish the truth from a lie may not improve the validity of their statement (see Chapter 16, "Errors in Children's Reports," for more details). Moreover, there is no research establishing that children who are warned to be truthful are, in fact, more truthful or less likely to make false reports. In the absence of clear recommendations from research or from local courts, the interviewer will need to make a judgment regarding the utility of discussing the truth with particular children and should be prepared to defend that judgment in court, if necessary.

The interviewer will also want to assure children that it is **acceptable to say they don't know or can't remember** the answer to a question (Geiselman et al., 1993). The interviewer may wait for or even try to set up a natural opportunity. For example:

I: "How old is your grandmother?"
C: "I don't know."
I: "I'm glad you were able to tell me you didn't know. You probably won't know the answers to all my questions. When you don't know other answers, will you tell me then, too?"

The interviewer may also instruct the child first, and then test his or her ability to follow the instruction. For example: "I will be asking a lot of questions today. Sometimes you won't know the answer to my question. I don't want you to guess. If you don't know, you can tell me 'I don't know.' So let's try it out: How many molecules are in this room?"

The interviewer will also want to **counter the child's assumption of adult omniscience** (Ceci & Bruck, 1993). The interviewer can explain that the child might have been there when something happened, but the interviewer wasn't, so the child will know and the interviewer will not. For example, "You said your birthday was a couple of days ago. I wasn't there, so I don't know what happened. What happened on your birthday?" After the child tells, the interviewer can emphasize that the interviewer may be ignorant of other events in the child's life as well.

> *The interviewer might want to encourage the child to notify the interviewer about language non-comprehension.*

Similarly, the interviewer might want to encourage the child to **notify the interviewer about language noncomprehension** (Walker, 1994). The interviewer could emphasize that he or she might use a word the child doesn't understand, for example, ". . . like flabbergasted—do you know what that means?" The interviewer can explain that there are some words the interviewer doesn't know either, and that it's OK not to know what a word means, as long as the child lets the interviewer know, so he or she can use a different word.

Some interviewers feel it is important to examine the child's ability to correct an adult. In many situations, the interviewer will make a mistake (e.g., mispronouncing a name, repeating what the child says but missing important details), and some children will spontaneously correct the interviewer whereas other children will not. Some interviewers choose not to await a mistake; rather, they intentionally make a misstatement, to examine whether the child will correct the interviewer (pointing to an elephant and saying "That one looks like a mouse to me. What do you think it is?"). Certainly, when the child is able to correct the interviewer, concerns regarding child suggestibility are somewhat allayed, and this process illustrates that the child has confidence in his or her knowledge. When a child is unable to correct the adult, the need for careful questioning is underscored. It must be noted, however, that the link between this sort of questioning and child suggestibility has not been researched, and it is possible that a child who corrects an adult in one topic area (e.g., misstating the child's age) may be suggestible regarding other topic areas (e.g., a poorly remembered event, such as a party 2 years ago), and vice versa. Thus, the children who pass this test may be suggestible regarding sexual abuse, whereas the children who fail the test may not be suggestible regarding sexual abuse.

14. SOMETIMES, IT MAY NOT BE POSSIBLE TO SET THE STAGE

It is important to note that some children will disclose promptly upon entering the interview room (e.g., "You know what happened? Daddy touched my pee pee!). With older children, it is acceptable to ask if that topic can be discussed after the interviewer and child get to know each other a bit. With younger children, it may be difficult to re-cue the child's memory, and the child may misunderstand delays as indicating that the interviewer is uncomfortable with the topic. Thus, at times, it will be impossible to accomplish the tasks outlined in this section, due to the child's presentation. If the child's attention span is long enough, critical concepts can be discussed after the disclosure, by asking the child if everything he or she told really happened, and assessing concepts the child used in the disclosure (e.g., inside/outside).

A similar issue occurs with highly distractible young children whose attention spans are not long enough to encompass all the foregoing issues. With distractible children, multiple sessions may be considered, so that all goals may be accomplished.

❑   *Practice Tips*   ❑

1. Suggestions for artful synthesis of developmental assessment and role definition

With felt-tip markers as the central activity. Ask the child to label all the colors.

I: "Let's talk about truth and lies (or real and pretend, or real and not real). This is James (draw a figure, or have a picture). This is Suzy. James says this marker is red. Suzy says it is black. Who is telling the truth?"

C: "Suzy."

I: "Good. Today I want you to tell me the truth. Will you do that?"

Ask the child to help you figure out how many markers you have by counting them. Then pick up three markers in one hand and one marker in the other hand. "Which hand has more?"; "Which hand has less?" Ask the child to watch you put three markers down, and ask which one you put down first, and which one last. Next, ask the child to put a marker on the table, under the table, in the Kleenex box, in the child's mouth. The interviewer can then emphasize that it's acceptable to say, "I don't know," and ask the child how many markers there are in the whole world.

Using a chart or other items around the room. The child can be asked to label the colors of items on the chart (or in the room), can be asked to count items on the entire chart or just one row of the chart, and can be asked if the items on the chart (in the

room) are real or pretend ("Is this a real lion, or a toy lion?").
The interviewer can ask which item is first in the row, and which
is last. All but one item on one row can be covered, and that row
can be compared with an uncovered row to examine "more
versus less."

Using the child's own body. The child can be asked to label the
color of clothing, hair, skin, and eyes. The child can point to and
name different body parts, and can be asked to put a finger on
the table, under the shirt, in the mouth, and so forth. The child
can be asked about an obscure body part (the trachea) in order
to emphasize the acceptability of saying, "I don't know" and to
emphasize that it's OK to communicate language misunderstandings. The child can be asked to hold up all five fingers on
one hand, while the interviewer holds up only one finger. The
child can be asked which is more/less. Mislabeling a body part
or the child's hair color can be used to examine distinctions
between the truth and a lie.

With older children (7 to 8 and older), many researchers
(Geiselman et al., 1993; Yuille et al., 1993) recommend that all
beginning stage goals be accomplished by conducting **practice
interviews about neutral autobiographical events** (a birthday
party or other holiday, a recent trip, a pleasant incident with a
family member). To some extent, these practice interviews are
useful with children of all ages. This approach allows the
interviewer to gauge the child's memory and ability to report
significant details. The process of telling the autobiographical
event provides an opportunity to work with the child to ensure
that the child informs the interviewer if he or she fails to
comprehend a question or doesn't know the answer. The interviewer can also emphasize his or her reliance on the child for
knowledge of the event, because the interviewer was not there.
This age group can be asked to define the truth ("What does it
mean to tell the truth?") but may not be able to articulate the
difference between the truth and a lie (Lyon, 1996).

2. Suggestions for handling incorrect responses during stage setting

At times, children will give incorrect responses to questions posed during the initial phases of the interview. In general, the interviewer is advised to attempt to diagnose the problem and to give the child a second chance before concluding the child does not understand the concept. For example, a child may answer a question regarding the truth versus a lie incorrectly but may be able to correctly answer questions about real versus pretend. Some children may not have a good grasp of colors but can use their own bodies to demonstrate understanding of forensic concepts (e.g., instead of "If I said this marker was blue, would that be the truth or a lie?" use "If I said this was your leg, would that be real or pretend?"; instead of "Can you put the marker in the Kleenex box?" use "Can you put your finger in your mouth?"). The interviewer must also be willing to accept that some very young children do not understand the relevant concepts (e.g., 3-year-old children may not be adept at gender distinctions). After trying a couple of alternatives, the interviewer should accept that this child may not understand an important concept and that the child's statement will be judged accordingly.

9

Posing Appropriate Questions

❏ Guideline

The interviewer should elicit as much information as possible utilizing open-ended questions that encourage the child to produce a free-running narrative. When necessary to ensure clarity, the interviewer can move along a continuum of questions (Faller, 1990a) from general to specific, using discretion in selecting questions that balance the goals of eliciting accurate information and facilitating complete disclosure.

❏ Supporting Information

1. QUESTIONS AS MEMORY CUES

Fundamentally, the task of the child interviewer is to help the child provide a complete and reliable account of events in the child's life, including abusive experiences. The interviewer's questions and tools can be thought of as memory cues employed to stimulate the child's recollection. Questions incorporate varying levels of cues, from general questions that provide permission to disclose with few cues regarding the type of information desired, to leading questions that provide significant cues regarding the interviewer's concerns about what may have happened to the child. The stronger the cue, the more information is provided by the interviewer rather than the child. As more information is provided by the interviewer, children's reports become more elaborate, but children also make more errors. Consequently, the stronger the memory cue, the less confidence the interviewer should have in the child's response. The issues of cueing, children's error rates in response to particular types of questions, and the types of questions needed to elicit a complete account of abusive events will be thoroughly discussed in upcoming sections of this guideline, as well as in the guideline in Chapter 15, "Memory and Suggestibility."

2. OPEN-ENDED OR GENERAL INQUIRY QUESTIONS ARE THE MOST DESIRABLE

Questions that invite the child to speak freely and spontaneously are variously labeled "open-ended," "general inquiry," or "invitational." These questions typically begin with the words "who," "what," "where," "when," "why," and "how." This category also includes prompts for more information, such as "Tell me more about that" and "Then what happened?" When asking an open-ended or general inquiry question, the interviewer gives very little information to the child regarding what the child should discuss, thereby reducing concerns that the content of the child's statement was influenced by the interviewer's beliefs and biases. Research studies of children who have not been abused consistently show that children's answers to open-ended questions are highly accurate, and as

> *Research studies of children who have not been abused consistently show that children's answers to open-ended questions are highly accurate.*

accurate as adult answers to similar questions, provided that the child has not been coached or misled prior to the interview (cf. Goodman et al., 1995; Poole & Lindsay, 1995).

Some good examples of open-ended prompts include "Why are you here today?"; "How have you been feeling?"; "Tell me about that"; and "What happened next?" (Faller, 1990a; Lamb, Hershkowitz, et al., in press; Stellar & Boychuk, 1992; Yuille et al., 1993).

When exclusively open-ended, or general inquiry, questions are used, children recall significantly less information than adults. The amount of information elicited using open-ended questions typically correlates with the child's age; that is, the older the child, the more information the child is able to retrieve (Ceci & Bruck, 1993). Young children recall a great deal more information when they are given cues to direct them toward relevant topics and cues to stimulate memories of significant aspects of events (Fivush, 1993; Pipe, Gee, & Wilson, 1993). In sum, while open-ended questions are desirable, in order to elicit a complete account the interviewer may need to use questions that cue the child regarding important topics.

3. A NOTE ON THE IMPORTANCE OF PATIENCE

Because children's cognitive skills and language fluency are less developed than those of adults, children require more time to process questions and formulate replies. It is therefore critical for the interviewer to pause after asking a question, and even after the child has given a reply, to permit the child to elaborate responses. When adults speak with children, there may be a tendency to move away from open-ended questions prematurely, because the child's processing time is mistaken for a lack of response to the question.

4. FOCUSED QUESTIONS GUIDE THE CHILD'S ATTENTION TO A PARTICULAR SUBJECT AREA

Focused questions provide some cueing information (e.g., the interviewer wants to discuss touching or is interested in feelings about different family members) but still permit a range of responses. For example, children can answer a question about being touched in a way they didn't like by discussing being forced to kiss

Aunt Matilda's cheek at the family reunion. This type of question provides the interviewer with the opportunity to ask the child about subject areas related to suspected events of abuse. Focused questions also can be used to elicit clarification and more specific detail regarding statements made during a child's free narrative. According to Faller (1990a), these questions can focus on **persons** (e.g., "How do you get along with your dad?"), **body parts** (e.g., "Who has a penis?"), **circumstances of abuse** (e.g., "What happens at bedtime?" or "Do you have secrets in your family?"), and **prior disclosures** (e.g., "Did you tell your mom about something that happened?" or "Have you talked with other people about touching?"). It should be noted that focused questions as defined by Faller (1990a, 1996a) include a mixture of open-ended questions and specific questions (see upcoming definition) related to the topic areas of persons, body parts, circumstances, and prior disclosures. For example, Faller includes "What do you do when grandpa babysits?" (open-ended) and "Did you ever see a man's pee pee?" (specific) in her definition of focused questions. See Figure 9.1 for more examples of focused questions.

5. MULTIPLE-CHOICE QUESTIONS PROVIDE THE CHILD WITH A LIST OF POSSIBLE ANSWERS.

Multiple-choice questions restrict the child's options to the ones provided by the interviewer. They provide strong cues regarding the type of answer desired but still leave the child a range of options. Multiple-choice questions are helpful when children indicate that something happened, but they are having difficulty providing details. Multiple-choice questions provoke concern because the answers are provided for the child. It is possible that a child will choose randomly from the options provided by the interviewer when the child does not know the answer or when the right answer is not included among the choices provided by the interviewer. This problem can be ameliorated if the interviewer ends multiple-choice questions by inviting the child to provide other options. For example, "Did it happen in the living room, bedroom, *or some other room?*" The interviewer can also improve the situation by utilizing a nonleading list, that is, by embedding improbable choices along with

Question Type	Example
Open, free recall, more confidence	
1. General Inquiry Question	Why did you come to see me?
2. Focused Question	
A. People	What kind of a guy is your dad?
B. Body parts	What is this (pointing to a part on a doll)?
	Have you seen one of those?
	Who has a pee pee like that?
C. Circumstances	Who babysits you? What happens at ___'s house?
D. Prior disclosure	Did you tell your mom about something that happened?
3. Follow-Up Question	
A. Narrative cue	What happened next?
B. Confirm disclosure	You said Grandpa touched you?
C. Clarification	Where did he touch you?
D. Details of abuse	What did that feel like?
	Did anything come out of his private?
E. Context details	Where did this happen?
4. Multiple-Choice Question	Did it happen in the daytime, nighttime, or both?
5. Direct (Yes/No) Question	Did Daddy touch your pee pee?
6. Leading question	Your mom makes you suck her breasts, doesn't she?
7. Coercion	You can't leave until you tell me what happened.

↓

Closed, highly cued, less confidence

Figure 9.1. A Continuum of Questions Used to Assess Possible Sexual Abuse
Reprinted with permission from Kathleen Faller, Ph.D. Slight modifications were made to the original figure provided to us by Dr. Faller. Dr. Faller approved our use of the modified version.

more likely choices. For example: "Did he touch with his foot, or his hand, or his private or his knee, or some other part?"

It is important to note that order effects have been found both with young children and with developmentally delayed children. Specifically, when these children do not know the answer to a question or when the question is incomprehensible to them, they tend to select the last option offered in a multiple choice list. This issue is less problematic if the interviewer remembers to use an invitational clause at the end of the question (e.g., "Was it daytime, nighttime, *or some other time?*").

In general, multiple-choice questions should be used only to clarify a disclosure. Faller (1990a) advises that use of multiple-choice questions be restricted to gathering

> *Multiple-choice questions should be used only to clarify a disclosure.*

information about context ("where" and "when"). Multiple-choice questions can be quite useful in gathering contextual information, particularly from young children. For example, "Was it before your birthday or after your birthday (Christmas, Fourth of July, etc.) or both?" or "Were you inside a building, or outside, or somewhere else?" Faller advises against using multiple-choice questions to gather information about the abusive acts themselves. In rare situations, multiple-choice questions may be used to gather information about abusive acts from an especially reticent child. For example:

C: "Grandpa touched me."
I: "Where did he touch?"
C: "I can't say."
I: "Was it on your face, or your private, or your hand or some other part?"
C: "The second one."
I: "Your private?"
C: "Yes."

It should be noted, however, that the interviewer in this situation could have also asked the child to point to the relevant body part on a drawing, on a doll, or on his or her own body. These other approaches would be preferable to using multiple-choice questions, because they do not restrict the child's options.

6. SPECIFIC QUESTIONS PROVIDE CUES TO THE CHILD

Specific questions provide information regarding both the actor (e.g., "Daddy") and the act (e.g., "touch you") within the context of the question. The child's range of possible responses is limited to yes or no. Relative to open-ended questions, the interviewer is providing more of the information, and the child is providing less. Therefore, specific questions are generally considered more suggestive than open-ended questions. In addition, a child may respond to these questions without understanding the question.

Within the category of specific questions, there is a broad range regarding the specificity of the information provided by the interviewer. For example, the name of the actor can be left open (e.g., "someone," "anyone") or can be quite specific (e.g., "Mommy," "Uncle Jim"). Likewise, the act embedded in the question can be located on a continuum of specificity ranging from rather open to quite specific, with many points in between, for example, "do anything you didn't like" versus "touch you" versus "touch your pee pee" versus "put his pee pee in your pee pee." As noted earlier, Faller (1990a) includes specific questions in which the actor and/or act are left open among her "focused questions." When the actor is left open and the act is not clearly specified, an affirmative answer must be clarified to identify the actor and to discriminate abusive from nonabusive acts (e.g., accidental touches, affectionate kisses, and hygeine-related touches versus sexual abuse). Open-ended questions can be used to clarify the child's responses (e.g., "Who touched you?" when the actor is unclear; and "Where did Mommy touch?" or "What did she touch with?" when the act is unclear). When specific questions leave open the actor and/or the act, and when they are followed by open-ended clarification questions, the child is likely to be providing most of the information. The series of questions involving open-ended prompts followed by specific questions followed by more open-ended prompts strikes a good balance between cueing the child's memory and focusing the discussion, while allowing the child to use his or her own words to describe what actually happened.

7. DIRECT QUESTIONS INVOLVE A
PARTICULAR ACTOR AND ACT

Faller (1990a) defines a separate category, labeled "direct questions," for those in which the actor and the act are clearly specified. Typically, the interviewer should not ask direct questions with both a specific actor and a specific action included in the question, unless the interviewer is confirming or clarifying information the child has already given. See Figure 9.1 for examples.

The interviewer should not ask direct questions that include a specific actor and action unless confirming or clarifying information already given.

It should be noted that among non-victim children, direct questions may be necessary to elicit reports of genital touch. With open-ended questions, up to 90% of children who have experienced genital touch will not report it. With direct questions, accurate reporting rates increase (70% to 85%) while the rates of false acquiescence (5% to 10%) and convincing, elaborated false reports (3%) remain low (Goodman & Aman, 1990; Saywitz, Goodman, Nicholas, & Moan, 1991). It should be noted that these authors moved from open to direct questions with the actor and act specified. It is not clear what percentage of children would have disclosed to specific questions with either the actor or the act left open. In other words, a less suggestive type of specific question might have been adequate for many children to disclose. It should also be noted that it may be even more difficult to elicit a report from a child who has experienced abuse than from children in research studies, due to additional barriers to disclosure for an abused child that were not present in experimental studies (e.g., getting a loved adult in trouble). Thus, in a typical interview, some specific and/or direct questions may be unavoidable, but the interviewer should quickly move back to more open questions whenever possible. For example:

I (Specific, focused): "Did someone touch your chest?"

C: "Yes."

I (open-ended, general inquiry): "I wasn't there, but I would like
    to know everything that happened. Please tell me everything
    that happened."

C: "He rubbed my chest."

I (open-ended, focused): "What did he rub your chest with?"

8. LEADING QUESTIONS AND COERCION
   SHOULD BE AVOIDED

Many experts on child interviewing (Faller, 1990a; Walker, 1997)
define leading questions as those that include an actor, an act, and
a tag (e.g., "haven't you?"; "didn't he?"; and "right?"). The tag can
occur at the beginning or at the end of the sentence. Such questions
are leading because a child is encouraged to provide a particular
response, usually an affirmative one. Coercion involves forcing
children to do or say something they clearly do not want to do or
say. Leading questions and coercion pressure a child to talk to the
interviewer and/or to give a particular type of response. The information gained from these strategies is not reliable, and these tactics
may adversely impact the child's mental health. Leading questions
and coercion are not acceptable approaches in child interviews.

Examples of leading questions include "Haven't you told your
mom about some touching?" and "I'm worried (your mom told me
she's worried) that your daddy put his pee pee in yours. Your dad
put his pee pee in your pee pee, didn't he?" An example of coercion
is "I really need to know what happened. It will be a lot easier for
everyone if you just tell me what happened." or "We can get popsi-
cles as soon as you tell me what Daddy did." See Figure 9.1 for more
examples.

9. A NOTE ON DISAGREEMENT AMONG EXPERTS
   IN THE DEFINITION OF QUESTION TYPES

In examining the foregoing continuum of questions, experts divide the continuum at different points and use the same terms to
refer to different subgroups of questions.

Some researchers on children's memory divide the question continuum into two categories: general and specific (Warren, Woodall,
Hunt, & Perry, 1996; Ceci, personal communication, 1997). General
questions are those that invite multiword answers and can be
answered with a range of responses. General questions are synony-
mous with open-ended questions, as defined earlier. These researchers are likely to include Faller's general inquiry questions and many
of her focused questions in the category "general questions." Specific questions include all other question types labeled earlier: some
focused questions (e.g., those that could be answered with a "yes/
no" response), multiple-choice questions, specific questions, direct
questions, and leading questions. Among these experts, all specific
questions are viewed as potential sources of contamination to the
child's memory. Within the specific question category, there is a
continuum representing how leading the question might be. These
researchers tend to use the terms *leading* and *suggestive* interchange-
ably. Specific questions are leading/suggestive to the degree that
they incorporate any information not previously provided by the
child and to the degree that they encourage a child to provide one
answer over another. In general, this group would agree with the
gradations listed in the foregoing definition of specific questions,
for example, that questions with an actor and an act specified are
more leading/suggestive than those that leave one or the other
unspecified. They would differ with this definition by being more
inclusive, that is, by also including some focused questions, multiple-
choice questions, direct questions, and leading questions in the
same category.

This group of researchers would consider all specific questions at
least mildly leading/suggestive, with some questions being more
leading/suggestive than others because they provide more information to the child and elicit less information from the child. It
should be noted that because this definition of leading questions is
so inclusive, most interviews are likely to include leading questions
as defined by this group of memory researchers. In fact, prior
research suggests that specific questions, defined as leading questions according to this group of researchers, may be necessary to
elicit complete reports from some children, particularly of genital
touch (cf. Saywitz, Goodman, Nicholas, & Moan, 1991). This defini-

tion also makes it more difficult for interviewers and reviewers of an interviewer's work to know when the interviewer has "gone too far." In other words, there is little guidance regarding which questions are suggestive but still permissible under some circumstances versus those that are unacceptable under any circumstances. An advantage of this approach is that it links the categorization of questions to research on children's error rates in responding to the question.

Faller (1990a), who originally described the continuum, defines leading questions by creating a clear boundary for practitioners, a "line in the sand," where any such questions would be considered highly risky and ill-advised (see Figure 9.1). Her definition of leading questions includes those that mention a perpetrator's name or an abusive action and those that command the child to acquiesce to the question (e.g., "Mommy poked your potty, didn't she?"; "Your dad rubbed your chest, right?"). Dr. Faller notes that as one proceeds down the continuum toward leading questions, the interviewer should have less confidence in the child's responses. Faller's specific and detailed question descriptions allow interviewers to locate questions on the continuum and track how close to the leading boundary they have come with a particular question. The detailed information is a rich source of guidance for the interviewer who is in a situation where open-ended questions are not working. In sum, Dr. Faller's continuum is widely accepted by practitioners because (a) it establishes a clear boundary for unacceptable questions and (b) it cautions the interviewer regarding multiple choice and direct questions but does not prohibit the interviewer from using questions that might be helpful to some children. In fact, Faller provides clear recommendations regarding when these questions might be useful and acceptable. It is very clear that interviewers should avoid leading questions as defined by Faller.

Dr. Faller also defines specific questions in which the actor and/or the act are not clearly specified as focused questions. For example, it was noted earlier that among "direct" or "specific" questions, there is a range regarding the specificity of the information provided by the interviewer. When the act and/or the actor is less specific (e.g., "someone" or "touch your body"), Faller would consider the question focused. When the information is more specific (e.g.,

"Daddy" or "put his pee pee in your pee pee"), Faller would consider the question direct.

These differing definitions represent a significant challenge to the interviewer trying to integrate research and interviewing practice. The interviewer must be conversant with both sets of definitions, must understand the distinctions between them, and must be able to translate terms. To the extent that the interviewer and other professionals (e.g., attorneys) reading the research lack any of these skills, they may misinterpret and misapply research findings. In addition, interviewers may be using one set of definitions for guidance in interviewing children but may find their work critiqued in court using the other set of definitions.

It should be noted that there are points of agreement between Faller and this group of researchers as well. Specifically, there is agreement that the interviewer should begin with open questions and only proceed down the continuum as necessary. There is also agreement that information obtained from specific questions is less reliable than that obtained with open questions, because children make more errors in responding to these questions. Both groups agree that specific questions vary in terms of their potential to suggest information to the child. There is agreement that many times, specific questions will be unavoidable, particularly with young children, but the interviewer should use caution regarding the timing and the wording of these questions. When using specific questions, interviewers need to realize that they may be challenged regarding whether the question was leading, according to the definition promoted by some researchers. The interviewer should be prepared to defend questions in terms of the child's emotional and cognitive abilities, and should be equally prepared to admit when a mistake has been made regarding an ill-timed or inappropriate specific question. The interviewer, and reviewers of the interviewer's work, must also realize that a single inappropriate question is unlikely to provoke a false report of abuse (Leichtman & Ceci, 1995; Price & Goodman, 1990; Rudy & Goodman, 1991; Saywitz et al., 1991; Tobey & Goodman, 1992).

> *A single inappropriate question is unlikely to provoke a false report of abuse.*

10. A PROPOSAL TO DISTINGUISH BETWEEN
QUESTIONS AND LEADING QUESTIONS

In response to the definitional conundrum detailed earlier, for the purposes of these guidelines, a distinction will be made between the terms *leading* and *suggestive*. The term *leading question* will be defined as Faller defines it, as including an actor, an act, and a tag (e.g., "didn't he?"; "don't you?"). When the interviewer's question includes information not previously provided by the child, the question may be labeled "suggestive." The more information provided by the interviewer, and the less information provided by the child, the more suggestive the question. According to this distinction, all leading questions would be suggestive, but all suggestive questions would not be leading. For example, mildly suggestive questions provide great latitude to the child in determining how to respond. For example:

I: "Does anyone kiss you in ways you don't like?"
C: "Yeh, my mom kisses my ear and it's wet. Yuck!"

It is important to note that **whether a question is suggestive depends on context.** If a child at one point in the interview states that her father touched her privates, it would not be considered suggestive for the interviewer to remind the child of her former statement. For example:

I: "You said Daddy touched your privates?"
C: "Yes."
I: "Which parts of your body are private?"
C: (points to front and back bottom)
I: "Which private did Daddy touch?"

Taken out of context, the interviewer's first and third questions might be considered suggestive, because they contain the name of an actor and a sex act. In context, these questions are not attempts to put words in the child's mouth but rather attempts to clarify the child's statements.

It is also important to note that **specific questions are not necessarily leading or suggestive.** For example, "Did someone touch your privates?" is a specific question, but an affirmative answer would require clarification about who did the touching, and further clarification to discriminate between abusive touch, accidental touch, and hygiene-related touches (bathing and toileting, genital exams). It is also important to note that specific questions are not always more suggestive than open-ended questions. For example, if a child states that his or her pee pee got hurt in the bathtub and is unable to respond to a question like "How did your pee pee get hurt?" then an open-ended follow-up question such as "Who hurt your pee pee?" is more suggestive than a specific question such as "Was anyone in the bathroom with you?" The open-ended question assumes non-accidental hurting and the presence of a perpetrator, while the specific question asks the child to provide information about whether anyone else was present. Similarly, the open-ended question "Where did Dad touch you?" would be acceptable following a disclosure but would be considered suggestive if it was the first question asked of the child.

11. MOVEMENT ALONG THE QUESTION CONTINUUM

The interview should always begin with open-ended, general inquiry questions that encourage a free-running narrative. While the child is supplying a running narrative, the interviewer should not interrupt or correct the child. The interviewer should also pause before posing more questions, to ensure that the child has the opportunity to fully elaborate responses to each question. The interviewer can offer encouragement for the child to continue the running narrative (backchanneling responses such as head nods or "Um hmm," or "What happened next?"). When a child has exhausted recall using these questions or is initially unresponsive to these questions, the interviewer should feel free to move to more specific questions. As noted earlier, multiple choice and direct questions are typically used only for clarification of prior statements. When used to clarify prior statements, these questions are not suggestive, because the child has already provided the information and the interviewer is merely seeking to clarify (Lamb, Sternberg, & Esplin, in press). If these types of questions are to be used to elicit the "who" and "what" of a disclosure, this should be done only after careful consideration, and it should be done in a manner that reduces suggestibility (see the section on direct questions for ideas).

Once a child provides a response to a multiple-choice or direct question, the interviewer should return to more open questions.

When clarifying the child's statements, the interviewer can move along the continuum from open to closed and vice versa as dictated by the child's ability to respond, and by the feasability of posing open questions. It is recommended that once the child provides a response to a multiple-choice or direct question, the interviewer should return to more open questions. For example:

I: "Did anyone touch your bottom?"
C: "Yes."
I: "Tell me more about that."
C: "Mommy touched my bottom."
I: "Where were you when that happened?"

This questioning algorithm—**(a)** beginning with open questions; **(b)** clarifying the free narrative with specific questions; **(c)** clarifying responses to specific questions with open questions whenever possible; and **(d)** using multiple choice and direct questions sparingly— is endorsed by numerous authors of interviewing protocols and standards (Berliner, 1990; Faller, 1996a; Home Office and Department of Health, 1992; Stellar & Boychuk, 1992; Yuille et al., 1993).

12. INTERVIEWING THE PRESCHOOL CHILD

Although the preschool age child is able to retrieve accurate information regarding an event through free recall, studies consistently show that a preschooler's account of an event will most likely be abbreviated (cf. Leippe, Romanczyk, & Manion, 1991). With open prompts, 3- to 4-year-olds report as little as 20% of what actually occurred. With specific questions, the same children recall up to 70% of experienced events. Likewise, studies show that nonabused children are unlikely to spontaneously report genital touch in free recall, even when it is documented to have occurred (Saywitz et al., 1991). Although the foregoing studies were conducted on non-victims, clinical experience suggests that a similar phenomenon occurs during sexual abuse interviews.

It should be recognized that when talking with a young child, the child will require more support from the interviewer in the form of cues regarding topic relevance, components of the event that are important to relate, and the level of detail desired (Fivush, 1993; Pipe et al., 1993). Thus, interviews with preschoolers are likely to include a higher proportion of focused questions, multiple-choice questions, and direct questions. Props such as anatomically detailed dolls and drawings may be helpful with some preschool children (see the upcoming chapter on the use of anatomical dolls for a discussion of the pros and cons of using dolls with preschool children of different ages).

Cueing a young child also raises concerns of suggestibility, particularly since preschool-age children are more susceptible to suggestion than are school-age children and adults (Ceci & Bruck, 1993). Young children may answer specific questions despite a lack of knowledge regarding a particular detail. The younger the child, the higher the likelihood of this problem (Ceci, Ross, & Toglia, 1987a). However, emerging studies indicate that when cue questions are neither leading nor coercive, compromises in accuracy are minimal (Goodman & Aman, 1990; Wilson & Pipe, 1989) and do not typically involve false accusations of abuse (Leippe et al., 1991; Saywitz et al., 1991).

As always, when interviewing the preschool child, the interviewer should begin with open questions and proceed down the continuum only when it is clear that the child's ability to provide a free narrative has been exhausted.

13. FLEXIBILITY

The interviewer should be flexible and able to use various types of questions, depending on the needs of the child and the dictates of the situation. For example, some studies (Dent, 1991) indicate that highly skilled interviewers produce very accurate reports even though they used very few open-ended questions and many specific questions. The interviewer should always keep the best interests of the child in the forefront when determining how to approach questioning.

The actual questions posed during an interview are important but may be ineffective unless presented in a skillful manner. Careful attention must be paid to the timing of questions and to nonverbal messages of the interviewer, as well as to the messages delivered by the child regarding the direction the interview should take. For example, older children might be cognitively capable of providing a running narrative but may indicate a reluctance to do so. In this case, it is very appropriate for the interviewer to offer children the opportunity to use tools (writing responses, anatomical dolls, pointing to their own body), and/or to respond to specific questions.

❏   *Practice Tips*   ❏

1. Eliciting a running narrative

Whenever possible, the interviewer should strive to elicit a free-flowing, running narrative from the child regarding what happened. What follows are some good narrative elicitation devices:

> "I wasn't there, but it is important that I know everything that happened. Can you tell me everything that happened, starting with how it began?";

> "What happened next?"; "How did it end?";

> "How do you know ___?"; "Tell me about him."; "What do you like about him?"; "What do you dislike about him?";

> "Why are you here to see me today?"

Following a disclosure, the interviewer could say, "Tell me more about that," or "What did you see/hear/feel during the touching?"

2. Asking about the first incident or the most memorable incident

When there have been multiple incidents, it is sometimes helpful to the child if the interviewer asks the child to describe the first time something happened, before probing other incidents (Morgan, 1995). For many children, primacy effects operate, so the first incident is a memorable one. In addition, the first incident may involve less serious acts and is more temporally distant for the child, both of which operate to keep anxiety at a manageable level. Moreover, beginning with the first incident can help establish a progression of abuse (grooming to fondling to intercourse). Such information is helpful to law enforcement regarding establishment of the perpetrator's motives and intentions. This information may also be helpful for the child's treatment provider, in evaluating the likelihood of cognitive distortions and the emotional impact of the abuse. It should be noted that the child will likely tell the first incident he or she remembers, which may not actually be the first incident.

Asking about the first incident would be useful only with children who understand the relevant concepts (e.g., first versus last). It is equally acceptable for the interviewer to ask, "Tell me about one time you remember" (after the child has disclosed touching) and assume that the child will tell about the most memorable incident.

3. Using script knowledge

Many memory experts note that when the abuse has occurred over a long period of time, the child may have developed a "script," which is a memory of "how it usually happens," including typical locations, how the perpetrator cued the child's participation, typical activities, how it would end, and so forth. These experts (cf. Price & Goodman, 1990) suggest that the interviewer attempt to elicit script knowledge before proceeding to discussions of other incidents. Script knowledge can be elicited using questions like "How did it usually happen?" and "Where would you typically be?" The recommended way to inquire about multiple incidents is to then ask about deviations from the script, such as other activities, other locations, or times when the activity was interrupted (e.g., someone came into the room). It is noted that preschoolers may be unable to "tag" script deviations in memory and may therefore be unable to provide clear answers to questions about different activities, locations, or times (Farrar & Goodman, 1992; Hudson & Nelson, 1986).

4. Cueing

If a child is unable to provide information when asked open-ended questions and/or provides ambiguous statements about a possibly abusive event, the interviewer may use more specific questions to cue a child's memory and thereby elicit more information. The following are some suggestions for cueing a child's memory:

- The child has disclosed abuse, but when asked where and when it happened is unable to provide contextual information. The interviewer can then ask any of the following questions: "Where did you live when the touching happened?"; "What school did you go to?"; "What grade were you in?"; "Who lived with you?"; "Was it before or after (any holiday or event of significance to this child)?"; "Did it happen in the kitchen, the bedroom, the living room, or some other room?"; "Was it daytime or nighttime?"; "Had you eaten dinner yet?"; or "Was it cold outside or warm?"

- The child has disclosed that someone touched him in a way he didn't like, but when asked where he was touched, provided no response. The interviewer could ask, "Were you touched on your nose?"; "Mouth?"; "Belly button?"; "Private part?"; "Leg?"; and so forth.

- The child has disclosed that someone touched her genital area but has not identified who touched her. The interviewer can ask the child to identify family members and/or other important persons in the child's life (day care providers, teachers, family friends) or can use a list generated during history gathering. The interviewer can then ask the child to tell something she likes and dislikes about each person. The interviewer could also ask the child directly whether any of the persons listed touched her or if it was someone else.

As noted previously, once a child has answered a cueing question, it is suggested that the interviewer return to the use of open-ended questions, that is, "Can you tell me more about that?"

5. Handling emotional responses during disclosure

When you begin to probe topics that are associated with abuse, some children will exhibit an emotional reaction. Other children emote as they begin a narrative or when the sense of relief hits after disclosure is completed. Emotional reactions include crying, fidgeting, hyperkinesis, and anger. Some children may distract the interviewer or try to escape the interview room (e.g., asking to go to the bathroom, saying they want to bring something to their mother).

It is recommended that the interviewer acknowledge the reaction verbally and ask how the child is feeling (e.g., "I can tell this is hard for you. I wonder how you are feeling right now?"). If the child is able to label his or her emotion, follow-up questions should address the source of the negative affect. The interviewer can also offer the child choices for making the interview process easier. For example, the interviewer can ask, "What are you afraid of" and discuss the child's fears. The interviewer can offer tactile comfort, "Would it be easier if we hugged teddy bears while we talk?" and can also suggest alternative tools such as simple figure drawings versus anatomical dolls. Finally, the interviewer can permit changes in seating arrangements such as under a table, or facing away from the camera. With an older child, the interviewer should consider offering choices to make it easier, even if the child is not able to specifically describe the source of the problem.

With younger children, it is important to identify emotional reactions early, before the child is significantly distressed. The interviewer can then "titrate" the child's anxiety, by asking some abuse-related questions, then switching topics to offer the child comfort, focus on the child's capabilities (drawing together), and/or focus the child on positive sensory experiences (softness of a bear, sweet smell of markers, pretty colors on the child's drawing or clothing). Moving in and out of anxiety-provoking topics allows some children enough control so that they are able to tolerate completion of the interview.

❑ **Cautionary Note**

TEMPTED TO ASK LEADING QUESTIONS?

Some circumstances will leave an interviewer tempted to ask leading questions (e.g., when a child has an abnormal exam but is not disclosing; when a child lives in high risk circumstances and there has been familial pressure to recant; if a child has disclosed extensively to other professionals but is denying during this interview). Even in these circumstances, the interviewer is strongly discouraged from resorting to leading questions or coercion. Leading questions and coercion may make it more difficult to protect this child and other children in the long run, because these tactics are viewed with extreme suspicion in the legal setting, where decisions about child custody and offender conviction are typically made. See Chapter 17, "The Nondisclosing Child," for a discussion of alternative approaches when a child is nondisclosing.

The Use of Language
in Child Interviews

❏ **Guideline**

The interviewer should utilize simple words and short sentences when questioning children regarding possible sexual abuse. With children under the age of six, the interviewer must be particularly mindful of possible linguistic limitations.

❏ **Supporting Information**

1. MUCH OF THE INFORMATION IN THIS CHAPTER
   WAS DERIVED FROM WALKER'S (1994) BOOK

2. AGE-RELATED GUIDELINES ARE NOT ABSOLUTE

   Walker provides age ranges for the acquisition of various linguistic skills, which are reflected in these guidelines. However, the reader should note that there is tremendous individual variability among children in age of skill acquisition, depending upon many variables, such as parents' educational level, language stimulation in the home, and child intelligence. Some children will acquire skills earlier and some later than the age ranges listed in these guidelines. For example, low socioeconomic status children may acquire some skills as much as 18 months later than the white middle-class children who have been the subjects of most research studies (Lyon, 1996). Individual variability is also likely in skill expression, depending upon individual children's responses to anxiety in the interviewing context. The age ranges are provided as an organizing framework, so that the interviewer will be alert regarding the issues most likely to be problematic for particular children.

❏ For All Children

3. SHORT SENTENCES WITH EASY WORDS IMPROVE COMPREHENSION

Regardless of the child's age, questions should contain one main idea apiece. Longer questions should be broken down into shorter ones with a single focus. Even high school and college age students are less accurate with complex sentences and difficult vocabulary (Walker, 1994). With preschool and young school-age children, the interviewer should strive for three- to five-word sentences (e.g., "Tell me what Sam did"; "Show me what happened"; "Where did Betty touch?"). This recommendation is made for young children because of their inability to process multipart and lengthy questions.

4. AVOID UNNECESSARY CLAUSES THAT COMPLICATE THE QUESTION

Examples of unnecessary clauses include "Do you remember" or "Can you tell me" at the beginning of a question and tags such as "didn't he?" or "don't you?" at the end of a question. One of the problems with these types of question is that they typically pull for either a "yes" or a "no" answer from the child, and if the child fails to elaborate the "yes/no" response, the interviewer cannot be sure that the child really understood the question. For the interested reader, Walker (1994) provides an excellent summary of the linguistic and memory operations entailed by the types of complex questions listed here. For example, some children will take the question literally as a yes/no question and will answer "yes" without elaborating. Other children will remember the event but will answer "no" because it is difficult for them to discuss the issue. The interviewer may therefore need to follow up both affirmative and negative responses due to lack of clarity. Follow-up questions to a negative response (e.g., "Is it hard to talk about, or is it hard to remember?") may be

The interviewer may need to follow up both affirmative and negative responses due to lack of clarity.

interpreted as leading in some forensic contexts, because the interviewer is not accepting a negative response. It is also difficult to phrase follow-up questions to a negative response in a way that a young child can comprehend.

Walker (personal communication, 1997) recommends saying to the child: "I'd like to know more about that. Tell me what you remember," "Please tell me what happened," or "I would like you to tell me . . ." rather than asking "Can you tell me" questions. "Do you remember" questions are often asked when the interviewer wants to remind the child of a particular context when asking the question. Walker suggests using a separate sentence to remind the child of the context, such as "You said something happened in the bedroom." This sentence could then be followed by a general inquiry question about that incident, such as "What happened in the bedroom?" Tag questions can be rephrased by removing the tag and reordering the words slightly (e.g., "Daddy hurt you, didn't he?" becomes "Did Daddy hurt you?" and "You said you were in bed, didn't you?" becomes "Were you in bed?").

5. AVOID THE USE OF "PASSIVE VOICE,"
   WHICH MAY CONFUSE CHILDREN

    a. Avoid: "when you were touched by Daddy."
          Use: "when Daddy touched you."

    b. Avoid: "Were you hurt by it?"
          Use: "Did it hurt?"

Direct phrasings are preferable to phrasings using passive voice. According to Walker (1994), preschoolers may misinterpret passives in terms of word order; for example, "when you were touched" equals "when you touched," and "were you hurt by it" equals "you hurt it." Passives are generally understood by ages 10 to 13, although some people do not acquire understanding until adulthood.

6. THE INTERVIEWER MAY WANT TO EXAMINE
   THE CHILD'S UNDERSTANDING OF TERMS

The interviewer may want to test the child's understanding of important terms to be used during the interview before questioning (see Chapter 8, "Setting the Stage"). It may also be necessary at times to directly question children about their usage of a term (e.g., "Tell me what a rod is," or "Where are your drawers?"). Body surveys using dolls and drawings are particularly helpful in defining a **common terminology for body parts.** This arena is especially important in sexual abuse interviews, given the focus on bodily victimization. In addition, studies have shown that children use many idiosyncratic names for private parts (Schor & Sivan, 1989), and many young children do not know which parts of the body are considered private (Goodman & Aman, 1990).

> *Many young children do not know which parts of the body are considered private.*

7. MAKE SURE THE CHILD IS ALERTED TO THE CONTEXT OF THE QUESTION

When discussing a particular situation (or person), it is good to alert the child and help the child stick to a discussion of that particular incident. For example, "Think about the last time Mommy touched you" or "I'd like to know more about when Daddy (vs. Uncle John) touched you." For young children, context reminders are always important. They are also particularly important with older children when there are multiple incidents and/or multiple perpetrators.

It is important to clearly inform the child when you are shifting from one event (or person) to another, or from the present to the past. For example, "We've been talking about when Daddy touched you in the bedroom. Now I want to know about the time in the bathroom. What happened in the bathroom?"

If you are asking a number of questions regarding a particular incident or location, it is helpful to remind the child frequently of the context of the questions. For example, "When you were in the bathroom, what did Daddy touch with?" or "So you were in the bathroom. Where in the bathroom?"

8. ON THE USE OF "WHY" QUESTIONS

Walker (1994) discourages the use of "Why" questions. When the question is about the respondent's motivations or intentions, the question is likely to be perceived as critical. These questions are generally phrased "Why did you . . ." or "Why are you . . ." There is a risk that the child will feel defensive when asked this type of question. The defensive feelings may interfere with the child's ability to answer the question, or the child may become focused on justifying his or her actions. In addition, "why" questions require a number of advanced cognitive skills, including self-reflection, recapturing past causal reasoning regarding motivations for actions, inferring other people's reasoning processes, and using language to describe these processes. Many young children will simply be unable to respond to such questions and will say, "I don't know," or will provide an illogical response. Children aged 7 to 10 may be able to answer "why" questions regarding their own behavior, and children aged 10 to 13 may be able to answer them regarding other people's behavior.

At times, the interviewer may want to know about the child's motivations and intentions, particularly when there is a concern that the child did not tell about the abuse because of threats or out of fear of the perpetrator. The interviewer can rephrase the question to remove the "why"—for example, "Was there a reason you didn't tell?" Walker (personal communication, 1997) notes that at times the word *what* can be used to rephrase a question and make it both less complex and less critical. For example, "What scared you?" versus "Why were you scared?" and "What did you think about telling?" versus "Why didn't you tell?"

9. SPECIFIC WORDS MAY INFLUENCE ANSWERS

Walker, in her book (1994) and in her presentations (1997), reviews a number of specific words that are frequently used in questioning children about suspected abuse but that are frequently misunderstood by children of different ages. Throughout this chapter, the words and the difficulties they pose for children will be presented. For a more thorough discussion, the reader is referred to Walker's (1994) book.

any: Requires a global memory search. Children may inaccurately answer "no."

the/a: *The* suggests a yes answer. Children may be more accurate using *a*.

not: In one study, insertion of *not* into a question increased inaccuracies of kindergarten through fourth-grade children by 50% or more. Error rates of ninth-graders and college students also significantly increased when the word *not* was inserted in a question.

❏ For Children 12 and Younger

10. ON THE ABILITY TO PROVIDE RUNNING NARRATIVES

In Anglo-American culture, narrative accounts of events have several expected components, including the setting (place, people, time), initiating action ("How did it begin?"), central action, motivations and goals, consequences/conclusion, and sensory descriptions. It is also expected that the story will be told in chronological order (Fivush, 1993; Labov, 1982). The narrative model that includes these components is taught in American schools, beginning in kindergarten. Parents teach the model to their children, through reading and by asking the children questions about events, which elicit components of the narrative model (McCabe & Peterson, 1991). While the ability to provide sketchy autobiographical narratives begins at age 2, it is not fully acquired until the late teens (Walker, 1994). Children are likely to provide narratives that are incomplete and disorganized by adult standards.

The narrative model organizes the account for the listener but also acts as an aid to memory storage and retrieval when events are experienced and recalled (Fivush, 1993). Younger children (who have not internalized this retrieval aid) will be more dependent upon the cues embedded in the questions posed by the interviewer in order to provide a complete account. Their accounts across interviews are also likely to be inconsistent, because of variations in the wording of questions, the context of the questions, and many other factors.

Different cultures have different narrative models.

It is important to note that different cultures have different narrative models. For example, in some cultures chronological order is a less important aspect, and in other cultures sensory descriptions are emphasized over actions. It may be difficult when the listener is from one culture and the speaker is from another, because the listener's expectations regarding how the account will proceed may be violated. This violation of expectations may be distracting, and the listener may be attempting to fit the account into a narrative structure that is different from the one used by the speaker in telling the story. I have had personal experience with children from African and European cultures in which the experience of feelings seemed to order the account rather than the sequence of events. Research on first-graders' autobiographical accounts indicates that African American children describe events in a series of loosely chained topics rather than in chronological order (Walker, personal communication, 1997). Interviewers should be mindful of this issue and adjust their expectations before interviewing children from different cultures. It may be necessary to ask more specific questions of children from other cultures, to elicit the components of the account that are important in Anglo-American culture and in the American legal system.

11. CHILDREN YOUNGER THAN 10 HAVE DIFFICULTY WITH QUANTIFIERS AND RELATIONAL CONCEPTS

The terms *quantifiers* and *relational concepts* encompass numerous skills. The age at which children have problems varies according to the specific skill (Walker, 1994). Preschool and school-age children frequently have difficulty providing reliable estimates of time (fully developed in teens); kinship (fully developed in teens); speed, distance, dimensions (size, height, weight; develops after ages 6 to 8); and quantity (e.g., all, any, more than/less than, some, each, specific numbers/amounts; develops into adulthood). Children under the age of 5 are spotty regarding accurate use of prepositions (before/ after; first/last; inside/outside). Superlatives (the most, the biggest, the best) are generally acquired by the age of 6 (Walker, 1994).

Walker (1994) cautions that many children will use these concepts in sentences before they are capable of responding to questions containing these words. Similarly, children can count before they can use numbers as estimates of quantities (e.g., how many times did it happen) and in a relational sense (e.g., five is more than three). Age ranges are estimates, and some children will acquire skills earlier than the listed ranges and some later. The interviewer may want to establish that the child understands these concepts if they are used to gather information regarding circumstances of abuse (see Chapter 8, "Setting the Stage," for examples). Alternatively, the interviewer can ground the child using names ("Bobby," rather than "your uncle") or concrete indicators (e.g., allowing children to use their own bodies during an exam or an anatomical doll to clarify inside/outside).

❑ For Children 9 and Under

12. SPECIFIC WORDS THAT MAY BE PROBLEMATIC FOR CHILDREN 9 AND UNDER

know/think/guess/sure: Adults use these to reflect gradations in certainty regarding knowledge. Children begin using *know/sure* versus *think/ guess* at age 4 but before age 9 are not reliable in making these distinctions.

remember: To adults, the word implies recollection of a fact. To children under 8 for 9, it may not imply knowledge of facts. To a preschooler, it may imply forgetting, then recalling.

13. CHILDREN MAY USE LANGUAGE THEY DO NOT FULLY UNDERSTAND

Concepts are acquired gradually, and children practice using concepts before the usage is fully mastered (Walker, 1994). For example, a child may use kinship concepts such as "Daddy," "uncle," or cousin without fully understanding the meanings in terms of blood relations (e.g., mother's husband, father's brother, etc.). Children aged 4 to 8 (and even older, sometimes) may use the terms *week*, *month*, and *year* without knowing what they mean (e.g., that there are 7 days in a week, 12 months in a year, etc.).

Alternatively, a child may not seem to understand conceptual distinctions (e.g., inside/outside or on/off) when using a marker in your office (a novel environment) but may be accurate in describing these concepts in an autobiographical account of repeated abuse. If one demonstration doesn't work, the interviewer is encouraged to give the child another chance. For example, instructing the child, "Please take **off** your shoe," "Put your finger **inside** your ear."

14. CHECKING FOR MISCOMMUNICATION

Miscommunication can occur at any age but is more common with preschoolers and young school-aged children. Children sometimes will not inform an interviewer when there is a misunderstanding because they may not realize they misunderstood the question (Walker, 1994). This can happen because of the natural power differential between adults and children and because the ability to monitor one's language comprehension develops in late childhood and early adulthood. When a child's answer seems inconsistent with prior answers or difficult to interpret, the interviewer should check for miscommunication. Common miscommunications include:

Children may interpret questions literally (e.g., touch doesn't include washing, poking, or rubbing; clothes are different from pajamas; apartments and trailers are not houses). The interviewer can ask separate questions regarding different kinds of touch/ locations/objects and/or can pay attention to the words the child used in initial disclosures to others and try those words first.

Children don't move well from the general to the particular. This phenomenon occurs for two reasons: (1) Their ability to search memory is limited; and (2) they don't group objects and events in the same way as adults. For example, a general question such as "Did someone touch you in a way you didn't like?" might elicit a "no," while a more specific question, "Did someone poke your pottie?" might elicit a "yes." The first question includes a higher order word, "touch," that children might interpret narrowly to mean a particular sort of contact with the hand (Walker, 1994). They may not realize the adult intended the word to encompass poking, rubbing, and so forth. The first question also includes a prompt for a global memory search, "way you didn't like." Young children may not be able to search their memory for all the touches they didn't like.

The question may have been too complex or poorly phrased (e.g., with multiple clauses such as "Can you tell me (1) where you were (2) the first time (3) you got touched (4)?"). Children may respond "no" to complex questions due to lack of comprehension. They may respond "yes" to please the interviewer but be unable to elaborate. Rephrasing the question may provoke a useful response (e.g., "Remember the first time Daddy touched you. Where were you?").

The interviewer should also be alert for **idiosyncratic word usage.** An anecdotal example best illustrates this concept. A young child disclosed that an uncle's friend touched his "stuff" in his "drawers." The interviewer inquired about this apparently unremarkable statement, and the child explained that he called his penis his *stuff* and used the word *drawers* to refer to underpants.

At times, children may lack the experience base to place an event in context, so they will **describe what something felt like rather than what actually happened.** For example, digital penetration or penetration by an erect penis may be described as "she poked it with a stick" or "he stabbed me with a knife." This metaphori-

> *Children may not realize they have misunderstood a question.*

cal communication can happen when the tactile sensations were most prominent and/or the child did not see what was happening. Children may not realize they are communicating metaphorically, and they may not signal the interviewer. Follow-up questions about actual experiences are helpful, for example, "Did you see what he poked with?" or "What made you think it was a knife?"

15. NAMES ARE BETTER THAN PRONOUNS

Children under the age of 7 have not fully mastered the usage of personal pronouns (he, you, me), object pronouns (this, that), and locatives (here, there) because these parts of speech require the child to simultaneously process the question and figure out what the pronoun is referring to. Children as young as 2 or 3 begin using these parts of speech, but their accuracy is spotty. So with preschool and young school-age children in particular, it is better to repeat names of people, places, and objects (e.g., "Where were you when Uncle Bobby touched?"; "Where in the bedroom?"; "What did Uncle

Bobby touch with?"). Repetition is less necessary if you can use pronouns to refer to something stated in the prior sentence or to something you can physically point at (e.g., if you've established that the adult male doll is Uncle Bobby and there was touching with a penis, then you can point to the penis and say, "Where did this touch?").

16. AVOID ASKING FOR DEFINITIONS OF ABSTRACT CONCEPTS, SUCH AS TRUTH

Most 5-year-old children can correctly identify truthful statements and lies when given examples but may not be able to provide definitions of "truth" and "lie." Most 7-year-old children can give a definition of at least one of these concepts but do not perform well when asked to articulate the distinction between the truth and a lie. With these age groups, the most fair and accurate approach involves concrete examples that permit the child to demonstrate an understanding (Lyon, 1996). For example:

Avoid: "What does it mean to tell the truth?"

"What is the difference between the truth and a lie (or real and pretend)?"

Use: "Let's talk about truth and lies (or real and pretend, or real and not real)."

"This is James (draw a figure, or show a picture). This is Suzy. James says this marker is red. Suzy says it is black. Who is telling the truth?"

Please note that the terms *truth* and *lie* could also be used in the rephrased example, especially with older children. See Chapter 8, for more examples.

❏ **For Children 6 and Under**

17. YOUNG CHILDREN HAVE DIFFICULTY REMEMBERING AND PROCESSING MORE THAN ONE IDEA

Responding to any question requires holding the question in short-term storage, searching long-term storage, and formulating an answer. Any question that requires even more operations will likely overwhelm very young children. This age group has particular difficulty with multipart questions and relational concepts (Walker, 1994). Just because they can count does not mean they can tabulate the number of times an event occurs (which requires accessing different memories, holding them in short-term storage, and counting them without concrete referents), nor does it necessarily mean they can accurately use relational concepts such as "more than/less than" (which requires holding two numbers and articulating their relationship). The interviewer is encouraged to assess the child's understanding of these concepts before using them to gather details of abuse with children 6 and younger.

18. CONSIDER EXPLORING "I DON'T KNOW" RESPONSES

This response might indicate a lack of knowledge, uncertainty regarding knowledge, or poor understanding of the question, or the child may be intimidated and anxiety may be interfering with the cognitive operations required to answer the question. The child may have also overinterpreted instructions to tell the truth (Saywitz, Moan, & Lamphear, 1991, as cited in Saywitz & Snyder, 1993). It should be noted that interviewers should accept "I don't know" as an answer, unless they have a specific reason to suspect a comprehension problem or affective interference. For example, if a child discloses digital fondling of the vagina, and the interviewer asks, "What did Sam do with his finger?" and the child says, "I don't know," the interviewer might be concerned that the child wasn't clear what information the interviewer was looking for and/or that remembering/reporting this level of detail is distressing to the child. The interviewer could follow-up with more direct questions, such as "There are different ways to touch: rubbing, poking, squeezing, patting. How did Sam touch your vagina?" or "Did Sam's finger touch on the inside of your vagina, or on the outside?" to clarify the "I don't know" response. When children answer "I don't know" to a number of questions, interviewers might try (a) rephrasing questions using simpler language, (b) switching back to rapport development before rephrasing the question, or (c) directly asking children how they are feeling and whether they are comfortable with the questioning. For example, if a young child is "bouncing around the room" and answers "I don't know" to several questions, the interviewer could focus the child's attention on a calming activity (playdoh, drawing) and then resume questioning.

19. CHILDREN'S ACCOUNTS TO DIFFERENT PEOPLE ASKING DIFFERENT QUESTIONS ARE LIKELY TO BE DIFFERENT (WALKER, 1994)

Children's statements will be inconsistent. The younger the child, the more inconsistent. Children have not yet internalized the cultural prototype "story model" that operates as an aid to both encoding and retrieval. They are thus more heavily dependent on adult questions, which may be different across different interviews. Children disclose more details with familiar individuals and in familiar environments. The interviewer's demeanor exerts a strong effect on the amount and quality of information, particularly with young children.

Children disclose more details with familiar individuals and in familiar environments.

Unfortunately, some people feel that inconsistency means the child is not credible. These individuals may not realize that the child may be referring to different incidents or different aspects of the same incident. Children may not be able to cue the interviewer when they are shifting contexts. It helps if the interviewer repeats contextual cues (see Section 5).

20. SPECIFIC WORDS THAT MAY BE PROBLEMATIC FOR PRESCHOOLERS

ahead of/behind: Used to discuss space and time. Children under 6 may misunderstand both uses.

ask/tell: Children may not distinguish them and may misinterpret *ask* as a command.

before/after: Children may get these confused. Answers to questions with these words may reflect whether the event happened rather than timing.

first/last: Children may use them fluently to describe events but may misunderstand questions with these words to age 5.

let/make: To adults, *make* implies force, but preschoolers mix these up.

more/less and some/all: Children under 6 aren't reliable at using these comparatively (e.g., *x* is more than *y*).

move and touch: These are higher order words (versus lower order words *wiggle, pull, go up,* etc., and *poke, rub, hug,* etc.). Young children may not have learned to include different sorts of movement and touch under these labels.

promise: Be careful of word order. Use "Do you promise to tell the truth?" rather than "Promise me to tell the truth," which implies that the child should promise that the questioner should be truthful.

yesterday/tomorrow: Preschoolers may use *yesterday* for all past events and *tomorrow* for all future events.

21. THE IMPORTANCE OF SPONTANEOUS COMMENTS AND RUNNING NARRATIVES, HOWEVER BRIEF

Interviews with preschool children necessarily involve greater numbers of direct questions. Unfortunately, research with non-abused young children suggests that some of them attempt to provide answers to any adult question, even if they don't understand the meaning and even if the question is bizarre (Hughes & Grieve, 1980; Moston, 1990; Pratt, 1990). Thus, children will likely produce a series of responses to a series of direct questions, but for some of these children the responses will be of questionable validity. The interviewer should make every effort to provide the child with opportunities for spontaneous comment: by asking open questions, by encouraging demonstrations, and by allowing the child some control over the interview process. When a child is providing little spontaneous comment, the interviewer should ask questions in different ways and with alternatives in different orders, to check for response biases and miscommunication.

11

The Use of Repeated Questions in Interviews

❏ Guideline

Once a child has responded to an interviewer's question, the same question should not be repeated.

❏ Supporting Information

1. A CAVEAT: QUESTIONS MAY BE REPEATED WHEN THE CHILD DOES NOT HEAR THE QUESTION

At times, the interviewer will be working with a distractible child, who does not hear the question or does not respond to the question due to distractibility. For example, if the child bursts into song in the middle of the question or if the child is engrossed in a project (drawing, Play-Doh) and makes no response to the question, the interviewer should attempt to garner the child's attention and then repeat the question. Research indicates that question repetition is problematic when the child makes a response, and the interviewer poses the question again. Under these circumstances, children may feel pressured to change their response.

2. REPEATING QUESTIONS WITH LIMITED RESPONSE OPTIONS INCREASES INACCURACIES

It is particularly important to avoid question repetition when the question is not open-ended and implies a limited number of response options (yes-no, and multiple-choice questions). Repetition of questions with a limited number of response options is potentially damaging to the credibility of the interview because research indicates that both children and adults may change their answers from accurate to inaccurate under these circumstances (see Ceci and Bruck, 1993, for a review). The intention of question repetition is typically to elicit an increase in accurate information or to clarify a confusing answer. However, in studies published to date, question repetition does not produce an increase in the amount of accurate information obtained from the interview (Ceci & Bruck, 1993; Poole & White, 1991, 1993). Furthermore, when repetition elicits a changed answer, the change is most often from accurate to inaccurate rather than the other way around.

It should be noted that researchers ask about events created as part of an experiment. These events may not be as well remembered as some incidents of sexual abuse (as with repeated abuse). Children who have actually been abused may be less likely to change answers because their memories are strong. Children who have not been abused may not be willing to admit to abuse to please an interviewer. On the other hand, if a child changes a response to a repeated question, which answer should the interviewer accept? Also, there are documented cases in which young children appear to have admitted to abuse to please a particularly persistent interviewer (see Ceci & Bruck, 1995, for a summary). The possibility of obtaining confusing and inaccurate responses suggests that repeated questions should be avoided.

3. QUESTION REPETITION MAY BE PARTICULARLY
DAMAGING WITH PRESCHOOLERS

Research indicates the adverse effects of question repetition are more pronounced with preschoolers than with other age groups (Poole & White, 1991; see Ceci & Bruck,1993, for a review). Because of weaker memories and developmentally appropriate desires to please adults, preschoolers are more likely than other age groups to change their answers based on demand characteristics of the interview, rather than on their own knowledge of events. Preschoolers are particularly prone to interpret repetition of a limited response option question as an indication that the adult is looking for a different answer (e.g., "Yes" rather than "No"). In fact, 42% of 5-year-olds have changed their answers in some studies, as compared with 21% of 6-year-olds and 10% to 15% of adults (Moston, 1987).

4. REPEATING OPEN-ENDED QUESTIONS
IS RISKY AS WELL

It is important to note that research suggests that repetition of an open-ended (general inquiry, focused) question is typically interpreted by all age groups as a request for further information, rather than an indication that an undesirable answer was given. Although open-ended questions may not provoke an undesirable change in responses, research evidence indicates that repetition of open-ended questions does not result in an increase in accurate information (Poole & White, 1991). In fact, when the answer is not known, or is unknowable, repetition of open-ended questions provokes speculation by the interviewee. Consequently, it is recommended that repetition of open-ended questions be minimized as well.

5. REPHRASING QUESTIONS PERMITS A CHECK
ON COMPREHENSION

Particularly with young children, the interviewer may be concerned that the child did not understand a particular question. This concern frequently arises when children's responses seem to be contradictory, when children are unable to elaborate on a response, or when children have a puzzled look on their faces as they answer a question. It is a good idea, particularly with young children, for the interviewer to be sensitive to cues that the child is not understanding particular questions. In these cases, the interviewer should rephrase the question with simpler language to see if the child's response changes.

6. QUESTION REPETITION SHOULD BE USED ONLY RARELY TO EXAMINE CHILD CREDIBILITY

Some interviewers directly examine child suggestibility and the presence of response biases (always selecting the last response to a multiple choice or yes/no question) by intentionally repeating questions with choices in a different order. These procedures are considered risky because of developmental tendencies (detailed earlier) for children to change their answers with repeated questions. This tactic would be acceptable only if the interviewer has good reason to suspect a response bias (e.g., the child does not respond to open-ended questions, and the interviewer has used many direct questions, and the child has tended to say "yes" or select the last option with multiple-choice questions). In addition, the interviewer must be mindful of the timing of the repeated question (e.g., preferably toward the end of the interview) and of the potential compromises in the quality of the information obtained. In general, it is recommended that the interviewer try to examine credibility using other means. For example, if the child says it happened at night, later in the interview, the interviewer might ask, "Did you eat dinner before it happened or after it happened?"

The interviewer should try to examine credibility using means other than question repetition.

❏   *Practice Tips*   ❏

1. Handling repeated questions when the full interview follows the child's exam

In some settings, the child is examined and briefly interviewed by the examiner. A specially trained interviewer then completes the questioning process. In these cases, it is recommended that the examiner's questioning be very brief and that the interviewer attempt to avoid asking the same questions. Many times, this is easily accomplished because the doctor asks direct questions in the context of a body survey, and the interviewer initiates the interview with a more open questioning process. Nonetheless, it is recommended that in these settings the interviewer and/or the examiner warn the child that question repetition may occur. For example, the interviewer can say, "My job is to find out everything that happened. I may be asking some of the same questions as the doctor, but I'll be asking lots more questions, too. If I ask the same question as the doctor, it doesn't mean you gave the wrong answer. It just means I'm trying to be sure I understand exactly what happened."

2. If a child gives a confusing response to a question, consider rephrasing the question

For example,

I: "Did Daddy touch your front private?"
C: "He kissed me."
I: "Who kissed you?"
C: "Daddy."
I: "Where did he kiss you?"
C: "On my front private."

or

I: "Where were your clothes?"
C: "In the drawer."
I: "What did you have on when Sam touched you?"

3. Suggestions for handling confusing or contradictory responses

When an interviewer is confronted with a situation in which a child provides an answer to a question that is difficult to interpret or that contradicts previous statements or information given to the interviewer, the temptation to repeat a question will be strong. In these circumstances, it is recommended that the interviewer:

- ALWAYS remain open to the possibility that the previously acquired information may have been false or misleading and therefore explore other possibilities with the child. For example, if a mother is certain a young child has been sexually abused by a noncustodial father, on the basis of the statement "Daddy hurt my potty," but the child is not making statements to you, you may want to explore bathing and toileting rituals and ask the child directly if anyone ever hurt her potty during bathing or toileting;

- Consider that the language used in the question was too complex for the child, and therefore rephrase the question using simpler language (e.g., "Did anyone ever touch you in a way you didn't like?" versus "Did someone touch you here?" pointing to a doll's private area);

- With very young children or very concrete children, consider that the wrong verb was used (*touch* versus *poke* versus *kiss*);

- With older children, try to rephrase the question in an open-ended fashion or directly address the confusing or contradictory information ("I'm confused. You said ___ and ___. Can you help me understand how those fit together?").

The reader is referred to Chapter 16, "Errors in Children's Reports" for other techniques and approaches to handling contradictory information.

12

Using Anatomical Dolls and Other Tools

Guideline

Anatomical dolls and drawings, as well as simple figure drawings, are useful tools for interviewing children who may have experienced abuse. Such props are most helpful when used as anatomical models and demonstration aids. Their use as cues to stimulate recall is more controversial.

Supporting Information

1. MANY USEFUL TOOLS ARE AVAILABLE

Anatomical dolls, nonanatomical dolls, anatomical drawings (Groth & Stevenson, 1990), free drawings (including, but not limited to, simple figure drawings; kinetic family drawings; drawings of places and/or instruments relevant to the abuse), and play therapy props such as telephones and puppets are commonly used in the interview context. See Appendix C for a list of sources for anatomical dolls and drawings.

In general, it is recommended that the interviewer avoid using play therapy props, because of the importance of maintaining the distinction between fantasy and reality in the interview context. When using any props, the interviewer should emphasize the "special job" of these props in assisting the interviewer in understanding "things that really happened." The interviewer should avoid using the words *play*, *pretend*, and *make believe* particularly when referring to props.

2. THE INTERVIEWER MAY BE CREATIVE IN THE USE OF NON-PLAY PROPS

The interviewer may want to test the child's understanding of several forensically relevant concepts, and it is often easier for a child to demonstrate an understanding rather than providing a verbal explanation. For example, the interviewer may want to use colored markers to help the child exhibit knowledge of more than/ less than (holding two versus four markers, "Which hand has more?"), inside/outside (of a cup, a Kleenex box, the interviewer's hand), on top of/underneath, and so forth. The interviewer can also use props or the child's features to demonstrate truth/lie distinctions (e.g., "If I said your hair is purple, would that be the truth or a lie?"). See Chapter 8, "Setting the Stage," for more information regarding these issues.

3. SIMPLE FIGURE DRAWINGS ENGAGE THE CHILD

Simple figure drawings, created by the interviewer and/or the child, give the child some control over the process of labeling body parts and are very useful in focusing the child's attention. For example, the interviewer can ask the child to draw a person or can have the child instruct the interviewer regarding what features to include, whether to draw a male or female figure, and so forth. In addition, the process of making the drawing provides ample opportunity for rapport-building and developmental assessment. For example, in assigning features to the drawing, the interviewer can explore children's likes and dislikes (curly versus straight hair, blue versus brown eyes), their knowledge of anatomy (elbows, knees, functions of different parts), the sophistication of their drawing skills, and, with older children, aspects of their body image (fat, thin, skin color, etc.).

4. ANATOMICAL DRAWINGS ARE VERY REALISTIC

Anatomical drawings are available in a series that includes different ages (young child, school-age child, teen, adult, older adult). The drawings reflective of different age groups have characteristic facial and body features as well as age-appropriate genitalia. These drawings are advantageous in allowing children to select a figure that accurately reflects their own development and in helping children specify characteristics of the perpetrator. By having the child fill in the perpetrator's features (hair color, skin color, developmental level), drawings may help with perpetrator identification when a name is not known or when there are two people with the same name. The genitalia are very realistic and allow for clear specification of parts involved in genital touch. Because of the frank presentation of genitalia, they lead quite naturally into discussions of exposure to nudity and pornography. These drawings are very useful in court, as a permanent record of the child's statements, particularly if the child participates in marking and labeling the drawings. Moreover, anatomical drawings have not been challenged in court, as have the dolls (Faller, 1996a, 1996b). Finally, drawings are less likely to provoke concerns regarding "pretend" and "play" than are dolls, because dolls are a standard component of children's play environments.

> *Anatomical drawings have not been challenged in court, as have anatomical dolls.*

5. MUCH OF THE FOLLOWING DISCUSSION SUMMARIZES APSAC (1995) AND BOAT AND EVERSON (1993)

6. DOLLS AND DRAWINGS HAVE MANY FUNCTIONS
   IN CHILD INTERVIEWS (APSAC, 1995)

Both dolls and drawings are useful **anatomical models** to assess child labels for body parts and to clarify confusing terms. They ensure that the child and the interviewer are using a common language when discussing functions of different parts and the events of an abuse disclosure. Both types of props may also serve an **icebreaker** function, by focusing the child on a discussion of body parts in a neutral atmosphere and possibly helping the child feel more comfortable discussing abusive events.

Due to their realistic construction and the representation of both child and adult genitalia, anatomical dolls and drawings may be uniquely useful as **memory aids.** Simple figure drawings may also be useful as memory aids, though they are less realistic. The sight of the body parts and questioning with relevant body parts in view may cue child memory in a way that questions alone cannot (see Section 7 in this chapter for a summary of research on the use of props as memory aids).

Dolls have additional uses. They may be used as a **demonstration aid** to allow a child to show what happened, when verbal skills are limited or are inhibited by anxiety or shame. Demonstrations can also clarify acts that are difficult to describe in words. Dolls are more useful than drawings in this regard, because they more readily permit depictions of interactions between two or more individuals, and they allow more clarity in demonstrating genital and anal touch, particularly penetration (Faller, 1996a; Steward, 1989).

Some practitioners advocate using the dolls as a **screening tool,** whereby the evaluator allows the child to freely interact with the dolls while being observed. The interviewer would then pose follow-up questions if sexually explicit play or comments are noted. This latter use is more controversial, because it elicits concerns regarding the distinction between fantasy and reality. Consequently, it is recommended only at the end of the interview and only in cases in which the child is nondisclosing (see Chapter 17, "The Nondisclosing Child," for discussion of less controversial options for handling nondisclosure).

7. A NOTE REGARDING RESEARCH ON THE
   USE OF PROPS

Numerous studies with nonabused children aged 6 and older indicate that props and specific concrete cues increase the level of detail reported relative to verbal cues or questions (Pipe et al., 1993; Steward, 1989). Reports with props are generally as accurate as strictly verbal reports for this age group, unless distractor props (items not present during the target event) are used in repeated interviews. When anatomical dolls have been studied as recall aids in interviews with nonabused children, the level of detail reported has doubled in some studies, whereas others have shown no increase in detail (cf. Gordon, Ornstein, Nida, Follmer, Crenshaw, & Albert, 1993; Saywitz et al., 1991). Although the amount of accurate information has increased with the use of props in these studies, increases in inaccurate information have been noted as well. False reports of genital touch remained rare (Salmon, Bidrose, & Pipe, 1995; Saywitz et al., 1991). Consequently, the use of dolls and other props as memory aids remains controversial.

There are two important limitations on the ability to apply research on tool use with nonabused children to interviews with abused children. The first is obvious: the memories of abused children and the social context of reporting abuse are difficult to replicate in a research setting (e.g., the emotional climate of the child's family, which may either support or discourage disclosure, is not replicated in research studies). A second less obvious limitation is also present. When interviewing children who may have been abused, there is a subset for whom **no event (e.g., abuse)** has occurred. Very few studies have examined the effects of props and cues on children being questioned about a target event that did not occur (e.g., a genital exam; Saywitz et al., 1991). It is hopeful that in the Saywitz study, rates of false reports of genital touch for the "no genital exam" group were low (0% with free recall and doll demonstration; false report errors increased only with direct questions). Our understanding of the usefulness of props in the forensic context would be best served by more studies comparing responses of event-present and event-absent groups of children questioned with similar techniques by interviewers unaware of which children are in the event-present versus event-absent conditions.

8. DOLLS AND DRAWINGS CAN BE VERY USEFUL WITH CHILDREN AGED 5 TO 7 (APSAC, 1995)

It is estimated that about 30% of all persons who have experienced sexual abuse are younger than 7 (Finkelhor, 1986). Young children produce highly accurate reports with free recall. However, studies consistently show that in order to elicit a complete account, young children frequently need assistance in the form of memory cues and guidance regarding topic relevance (Pipe et al., 1993; see Chapter 15, "Memory and Suggestibility," for more discussion on this issue).

An estimated 30% of all persons who have experienced sexual abuse are younger than 7 years old.

Young children are more likely to use idiosyncratic language and imprecise terms for body parts. Dolls and drawings can help ensure a common language regarding body parts, focus the discussion on touches and hurts to different parts, and cue children's memory regarding events with their own bodies. In some studies, dolls have been found to be particularly helpful in increasing the level of detail reported by 5- to 7-year-old abused and nonabused children (Leventhal, Hamilton, Rekedal, Tebano-Micci, & Eyster, 1989; Saywitz et al., 1991). In other studies, the effects of dolls on reports by 5-year-old children were neither facilitative nor detrimental (Goodman & Aman, 1990; Gordon et al., 1993). It should be noted that when increases in detail have been noted, children's inaccuracies have also increased slightly.

9. USE CAUTION WHEN INTERVIEWING CHILDREN AGES 4 AND YOUNGER USING PROPS

Many children under the age of 4 are concrete in their thinking and may not be able to use the dolls or other props as representations of reality (DeLoache, 1995). Because young children are not proficient at monitoring task comprehension, they may experience difficulty with the dolls but may not cue the interviewer regarding their difficulties. The interviewer can examine children's ability to utilize the dolls as representations by having children point to different features on their own and the doll's body and by asking children in what ways the dolls are similar and dissimilar to themselves, as well as to the alleged perpetrator.

In cases in which the interviewer has established that a young child can use a doll or other prop as a representation of reality, concerns remain regarding the usefulness of dolls with this age group. Some studies suggest that dolls increase production of accurate information with 3-year-olds (see APSAC, 1995, and Boat & Everson, 1993, for reviews), whereas other studies indicate that dolls do not increase reported information for this age group (Gordon et al., 1993; Salmon et al., 1995). Moreover, when props are used with leading questions to interview 3-year-old children about bodily touch, high rates of false reports of genital touch (i.e., 50%) have been observed (Bruck, Ceci, Francoeur, & Renick, 1995).

10. ANATOMICAL DOLLS ARE UNLIKELY TO PROMOTE SEXUALIZED FANTASY PLAY

In samples of nonabused children, there is little empirical evidence that dolls promote sexual fantasies and sexualized play (see APSAC, 1995, and Boat & Everson, 1993, for summaries). As noted earlier, when used as recall aids in interviewing children over the age of 4 about known events, dolls have been associated with increases in reports of accurate details and a low rate of false reports of genital touch.

11. A NOTE ON THE NEED FOR MORE RELEVANT RESEARCH ON DOLLS AND OTHER TOOLS

The original purpose of the dolls was to assist children with limited verbal skills, yet studies have questioned the utility of dolls with 3- to 4-year-olds. Some of the phenomena reported in research studies have been observed clinically in interviews of abused children by members of the committee that authored these guidelines (e.g., children being unable to use the dolls to represent themselves, children looking at how the doll is dressed and reporting that this is how they and/or the perpetrator were dressed). These observations, paired with the research findings, lead this committee to agree with recommendations that caution be used in interviewing 3- to 4-year-old children with anatomical dolls.

Research with children age 5 and older is mixed regarding the utility of the dolls (i.e., some studies support doll use, and others find negligible effects of doll use). Some researchers (cf. Ceci & Bruck, 1995) have labeled children 5 and over "verbally competent" and recommend that dolls not be used with this age group, because evidence for doll utility is mixed, and some evidence invites concern regarding doll suggestibility. We take issue with this recommendation, both on the basis of existing research and on the basis of clinical experience. In reviewing the research, there is not yet a convincing body of research that doll-induced suggestibility is a problem for the 5-and-older age group. Clinically, in many interviews, 5- to 9-year-old children have difficulty in verbally describing the spatial relations of sexual positioning. Although the interviewer would like clear statements such as "We were laying beside each other, and he was behind me" or "I was on top of him, he was sitting up, we were facing each other and I was sitting on his lap," children are frequently able to provide only a portion of this information (e.g., "he was on top of me," which for some children may mean he was standing over them). Children's reports may even appear contradictory or inconceivable due to limitations in their descriptive abilities. For example:

C: "He poked my bottom with his pee pee."
I: "Where was he?"
C: "He was standing up."
I: "Where were you?"
C: "Lying down."

This report was made by a child who could not verbally describe himself kneeling on his knees on the bed, with the perpetrator standing behind him (the child was able to illustrate this positioning using dolls and a bench located in the interviewing room). In interviews with children alleging sexual abuse, dolls seem to be very valuable as a **demonstration aid** in helping the child illustrate sexual position- ing. In this context, the dolls are typically used after a verbal disclo- sure of sexual abuse has been made, and they are introduced just at the point at which the child needs assistance in communicating. At times, the doll positioning can clarify whether the touch was abusive or nonabusive, and dolls provide information regarding the child's experience with sexual positioning (versus being told about these activities). We do not know of research comparing verbal and tool- aided reports of complex spatial relations and body positioning for children 5 and older.

Another very useful clinical application of tools involves **ensur- ing common terminology.** In our experience children have used unusual labels for private parts (e.g., "brontosaurus" for a man's penis; "cootchie cat" for a girl's vagina). At times, it is difficult or embarrassing for a child to indicate what the referent is for the term, either by pointing to his or her own body or responding to a question such as "What is a (unusual label)?" Once the interviewer ascertains that the referent is a body part, the child may be willing to point to the part on a drawing or doll. This use is particularly clarifying when the dolls/drawings are anatomically correct. Some inter- viewers prefer to use non-anatomical drawings and invite the child to either point to the location of the part or add it to the drawing. These sorts of clarifications are frequently necessary after a disclo- sure has occurred (e.g., he touched my "cootchie cat" with his "brontosaurus"). This issue has been overlooked in extant research.

Finally, the **icebreaker function** has not been well researched. Neutral, matter-of-fact discussions of body parts, their functions, and problems with different parts may help reticent or modest children feel comfortable with the topic. One study appears to support the use of dolls to help children disclose genital touch (Saywitz et al., 1991), but in this study the effects of direct question- ing—for example, "Did the doctor touch your privates?"—were not consistently separated from the effects of doll use (e.g., the direct question was asked while pointing to the private parts of a doll). Of

course, the use of dolls in an icebreaker capacity could promote
suggestibility as well. The critical concern is that there is currently
not enough information on these important issues of doll use in the
forensic context.

12. INTERPRETING CHILD BEHAVIOR WITH THE DOLLS

Studies show that it is rare for nonabused children to engage in
explicit sexualized play with the dolls (see APSAC, 1995, and Boat
& Everson, 1993, for reviews). That is, penile insertion in vaginal,
anal, or oral openings, mouthing a doll's penis, or simulating vaginal, anal, or oral intercourse between the child and a doll should be
a source of considerable concern to the interviewer. However, these
behaviors in the absence of verbal disclosure do not necessarily
mean that sexual abuse has occurred, because research studies show
that a small percentage of nonabused children will engage in similar
behaviors. Whenever a child exhibits such behavior in the absence
of a disclosure, the interviewer should carefully examine sources of
sexual knowledge for that child (pornography, witnessing adults or
older siblings, cable television, or sexual abuse). On the other hand,
manual exploration of a doll's genitalia, including inserting a finger
in the doll's vaginal or anal openings, is only a source of concern
when accompanied by verbal indicators, aggressive behavior, distress, or attempts to conceal the behavior. Exploration with neutral
affect is common among nonabused children.

❏   *Practice Tips*   ❏

1. It is helpful for the interviewer to be aware of prior exposure to interview tools

It is particularly important for the interviewer to know if the
child has been exposed to these tools in treatment settings in
which fantasy play may have been encouraged. When gathering the history, the interviewer should inquire regarding tools
used by previous interviewers. When a therapist is already
involved with the child, it is helpful to contact and question

that person regarding the child's exposure to anatomical dolls and drawings. Some research on nonabused children's interactions with props indicates that inaccuracies increase when props are used repeatedly to question children (Pipe et al., 1993).

2. Introducing anatomical dolls and drawings

It is often helpful to prepare the child regarding the realistic nature of these props. The interviewer can say something like "These dolls have all of their body parts just like real people, even the parts under the clothes"; or "My pictures look just like we do when we get out of the bath."

The interviewer may also want to introduce dolls and drawings in a way that facilitates the child's use of these tools as representations of reality. For example, Morgan (1995) suggests that when children are selecting a doll, it is helpful to ask them something like "I want you to pick one doll to *be* you, and a different doll to *be* (alleged perpetrator, if the child has identified the perpetrator)." As noted earlier, children can customize drawings, by coloring hair, eyes, and skin to match themselves and/or the alleged perpetrator.

3. It is helpful to have the child identify important characteristics of dolls/drawings

When anatomical dolls/drawings are initially presented, it is often a good idea to have the child attempt to discriminate adults from children ("Can you point to the drawings of grown-ups?"), and males from females ("Which ones are boys?"). Similar questions regarding the child's own age, gender, and skin color, as well as those of the perpetrator (if the child has already disclosed), are also helpful. These questions lay the groundwork for children to select an appropriate doll or drawing to represent both themselves and the alleged perpetrator, and are useful in avoiding difficult moments such as when children disrobe a doll, discover adult sexual parts, and are uncomfortable continuing to use the doll to represent themselves.

Of course, some children will select a nonrepresentative tool despite these precautions, and in these circumstances, the interviewer can provide the child with the opportunity to select another doll. For example, "Does that body look like yours?"; "How is it the same/different?"; and "Would you like to use a different doll?" Even after noting the discrepancies between the doll or drawing and themselves, some children will persist in using an unrepresentative tool. This should be permitted, because children may be focused on other characteristics that are important to them but perhaps less obvious to the interviewer (hair color, bigger size for a feeling of power, etc.).

4. Interview tools can provide the child with emotional distance

Dolls and drawings may be used to provide a child with emotional distance, thereby reducing the intensity of the disclosure process for the child. As noted earlier, pointing to body parts involved in the abuse by pointing to the part on a doll or drawing may be less stressful than pointing to the same part on the child's own body. Similarly, the child may want to use his or her own name to refer to the doll in the third person (e.g., Susie might say, "Then Susie put her hand on his pee pee"). This device is useful, because it may provide the child with some emotional distance. Speaking in the third person can be established by the interviewer with young children who might benefit from emotional distance (e.g., "I want you to pick a doll to be Susie"). When doing this, the interviewer should check with the child every so often to clarify whom the doll represents (e.g., I: "Who is Susie?" C: "Me!").

5. Ideally, dolls and drawings are used after verbal disclosure of abuse (APSAC, 1995)

Anatomical dolls and drawings are least suggestive, and most useful as recall and demonstration aids, when presented after the child has already made some disclosure.

After initially presenting the tools and having the child select representative tools, the interviewer should encourage free recall by having the child recreate the circumstances (location, positioning of clothing, positioning of dolls relative to one another, etc.), and then ask the child to show or tell "everything that happened."

6. Helping a child name and focus on genitals

With reticent children, it is acceptable to ask the child to name nongenital and genital body parts using the dolls and drawings, thus using them as icebreakers and memory aids. In one study, 75% of children whose genitals were touched during a pediatric exam disclosed only when the interviewer pointed to a doll's genitals and asked "Did the doctor touch you here?" (Saywitz et al., 1991). If such direct questions are asked about genitals in a forensic interview, similar questions should be asked about other body parts (e.g., "Did anyone touch your arm? Did anyone touch your face?"). A series of direct questions allows the interviewer to assess response biases (always saying "yes"), perseveration (always accusing one person of every possible act), and the child's ability to elaborate on affirmative responses.

Some children will be avoidant of the genitalia. This type of reaction may be more likely with realistic props such as anatomical dolls and drawings. In these cases, the interviewer can provide normalizing comments, such as "This is just another part of the body, just like the eyes, arms, legs," or "I've heard lots of names for these parts, so you don't have to worry about embarrassing me," or "This is a place where you can use any names you want and you won't get in trouble," or "I talk to lots and lots of kids, and other kids have told me it's hard (embarrassing) to talk about these parts. Is there a way I can make it easier?" These types of comments are most effective when stated in a neutral, calm tone of voice. If the child's discomfort persists, the interviewer should be willing to abandon use of the prop or switch props to help the child feel more comfortable.

7. The utility of free play with the dolls

Sometimes children will begin to freely manipulate and move the dolls after they've made one or more disclosures. They may make these movements without accompanying statements. The interviewer should permit this behavior, because it may be very helpful in establishing additional incidents or peripheral detail. However, the interviewer should prompt the child to provide verbal descriptions of what is occurring (e.g., "What's happening there?"). It is also important to ask follow-up questions, rather than making assumptions that these activities happened or happened with the same perpetrator (e.g., "You showed his pee pee touching her mouth. Did that happen to you? Who did that to you?").

8. When a child is physically aggressive with a tool

At times, a child may begin to tear up a drawing, scribble on a drawing, or hit a doll. If the child is going to destroy or harm the tool, the interviewer should comment in an accepting manner on the emotion but stop the behavior (e.g., "I can see that you're mad right now, but I can't let you tear up that drawing"). If the behavior is not destructive (e.g., hitting but not ripping a doll), the interviewer could permit the behavior and acknowledge it verbally (e.g., "I see you hitting the doll's pee pee. I wonder how you are feeling right now"). It is helpful to let the child know that feelings of anger, confusion, or frustration are normal, and that you've known other children who have felt the same way (Morgan, 1995).

9. Selection of tools is the interviewer's personal decision

The interviewer should develop familiarity with all available tools. However, the selection of particular tools may depend on the interviewer's comfort level or style. In many evaluations, the interviewer may not use any tools. Older children are unlikely to need tools, and research is not clear regarding the benefits of tools with the youngest age groups. When tools are used, there is no research suggesting that one tool is inherently superior to any others, and the tools have complementary advantages and disadvantages.

**10. The interviewer should feel free to use more than
one tool in a single interview**

Dolls and drawings have complementary advantages and disadvantages. Drawings allow the child more control and can be personalized; dolls allow more accurate demonstrations, particularly of acts involving penetration. The interviewer may use no tools at all in many interviews, or only a single tool, or may start with drawings, and proceed to the dolls if the child needs to demonstrate penetration or interactions among multiple people. The interviewer should make clinical judgments about what, if any, tools will be most useful to a given child.

❏ **Cautionary Notes**

1. INTERVIEWERS SHOULD AVOID LEADING QUESTIONS,
ESPECIALLY WHEN USING DOLLS

Research indicates that suggestibility effects may be enhanced when young children (under 4) are exposed to leading questions using props such as dolls (Bruck et al., 1995). Only when dolls are used with very young children in the context of leading and misleading questions have dolls been associated with high rates of false reports. In this context, the questions, procedures, and language limitations may have accounted for much of the suggestibility effect.

2. SOME CHILDREN MAY BE INTIMIDATED OR EMBARRASSED
BY ANATOMICAL DOLLS OR DRAWINGS

For some children, the realistic construction of the anatomical dolls and drawings may be difficult because the frank presentation of genitalia may be embarrassing. In addition, the process of demonstrating acts of abuse may provoke overwhelming memories and intense emotions. The interviewer should use clinical judgment regarding the use of tools and should check with the child regarding his or her comfort level with tools in the interview situation. If a child indicates discomfort, the interviewer should explore ways to help the child feel more comfortable and should stop using the tool if discomfort persists.

Ending the Interview

❏ Guideline

Once all available information has been gathered, the interviewer should give the child the opportunity to ask questions and should make an effort to end the interview on a positive note.

❏ Supporting Information

1. THE CLOSING COMPONENT OF THE INTERVIEW SHOULD BEGIN WHEN:

A. The Interviewer Has Checked With the Multidisciplinary Team

A unique advantage of the evaluation center interview is that the child is interviewed by one person while professionals from different disciplines observe. The interviewer can depend on input from these observers who may notice something significant that the interviewer misses or overlooks. The interviewer should use the knowledge and expertise of these professionals to ensure that the maximum amount of clear information is obtained in the most sensitive manner possible.

B. The Interviewer Has Obtained All Available Information

The interviewer should attempt to answer the basic forensic questions (Who, What, Where, and When) regarding any allegations of abuse. Some children will be unable to provide all components. The interviewer should mentally check that he or she has attempted to address these issues and can choose to end the interview when the child has provided the information and/or it is clear that the child is unable or unwilling to provide particular pieces of information. The interviewer should also check for other perpetrators and may wish to explore exposure to other risk factors (pornography, excessive discipline, domestic violence, pet abuse, safety of siblings or other children, and drug and alcohol abuse).

C. The Child Is Unable or Unwilling to Continue the Interview

When a child is indicating (verbally or nonverbally via signs of impatience or fatigue) that he or she would like to terminate the interview, the interviewer should explore explanations for the child's behavior and then take appropriate action. For example, the child may be avoidant of a particular topic or emotionally unable to relate details of an incident. In these cases, a treatment referral may be needed. At other times, as when children are tired or their attention span has been exhausted, a multiple session format could be considered.

Regardless of whether all relevant information has been obtained from a child, the interview should be brought to a close if that is what the child needs. Pressuring a child to continue when the child is unable or unwilling to do so may result in adverse mental health impacts for the child or may provoke the child to make inaccurate statements.

2. THE CLOSING COMPONENT OF AN INTERVIEW SHOULD TYPICALLY INCLUDE:

A. An Opportunity for the Child to Ask Questions

The interviewer should answer questions openly and honestly, providing the child with an answer, without overwhelming the child with details. When a child asks about "what will happen now," whenever possible, the interviewer should provide a minimal answer (e.g., "you'll be going home with your mom, and the police will be deciding what to do about your dad") and defer to other multidisciplinary team members ("If you would like to talk with Detective Bob, he can tell you more about what he will do"). The child should be given realistic feedback ("I think you will be staying in your foster home until your caseworker and your mother can work out a safety plan. Your caseworker is here if you want to talk with her about her plans"). The interviewer should avoid making promises about the future. There are no guarantees regarding the outcome of any given case, and thus no guarantees that a promise can be kept.

B. Thanking the Child for His or Her Participation

Whether or not a child has disclosed and irrespective of concerns regarding the validity of the child's statements, the interviewers should let the child know that they appreciated the child's willingness to talk with them (e.g., "Thank you for coming to talk with me today"). This component is important because it conveys that what the child had to say was important. At times, the interviewer may want to acknowledge that the conversation was difficult for the child (e.g., "Sometimes it looked like it was hard for you to talk to me today. I appreciate you answering my questions even though it was hard at times").

C. Transition into Positive Topics

Discussing topics that interest the child permits transition into a neutral or positive affective state. Hobbies, sports, or pets are often good subjects, as are the child's plans for the rest of the day. Returning to issues discussed in the developmental assessment and/or discussions of the child's artwork during the session are also good transition devices. Treats given at the end of the evaluation are particularly effective transition devices for young children (see the "Practice Tip" in this chapter for more discussion).

It is important to note that transition may be very short for some children and/or may occur as you are walking the child back out into the waiting room (as with the young child standing by the door as soon as you say you're done asking questions). Some children may be willing to disclose, but may find the interview process aversive and may just want the interviewer to get the facts and leave them alone (some adolescents present in this manner).

> *The interviewer should permit longer transitions whenever possible.*

With other children, the transition may be quite long, if they have many questions, if they are emotionally distraught, or if they need to complete a piece of artwork. The interviewer should permit longer transitions whenever possible. If the child is working on art but not talking with the interviewer, the interviewer may encourage the child to complete the artwork in the waiting room while the interviewer debriefs with the parents or multidisciplinary team.

3. OPTIONAL CLOSING COMPONENTS

A. Validity Checks

Some researchers recommend **reviewing the child's statements** to check for accuracy (e.g., "I'm going to tell you back what you just told me. Tell me if I say something wrong"). After such a review, children are often asked if there is anything they forgot to tell the interviewer. Children may be given the opportunity to **add to their statements** (e.g., "Is there anything else you would like to tell me

about right now?"). With children school age and older, these techniques can be effective in improving information coverage. However, the opportunity to add information
at times may be viewed as an invitation to
speculate. The perception that the child is
invited to speculate can be very problematic in court (Walker, personal communication, 1997). With young children, or particularly distraught children, the review
may be overwhelming. As a consequence,
these techniques should be used with discretion.

> *The end of the
> interview is often
> the best time to
> address concerns
> regarding errors in
> child reports.*

The end of the interview is often the best time to address concerns
regarding **errors in child reports.** It is also the best time to ask
forensically **risky questions.** See the guidelines in Chapter 9,
"Posing Appropriate Questions," and Chapter 16, "Errors in Children's Reports," for complete discussions of these topics.

B. Risk Factor Questioning

Some interviewers routinely ask about risk factors other than
child abuse, others ask only when the history indicates reason for
concern (e.g., police or parent reports of domestic violence in the
home, but the parent asserts that the child never witnessed or
overheard the violence), and others defer to treatment providers and
child protection workers to gather this information. Questions could
be asked about exposure to physical abuse or harsh punishment,
pornography, drug and alcohol abuse, pet abuse, or the impact of
parental divorce/separation on the child. These topics should be
addressed using the same questioning algorithm as for questions
about sexual abuse (see Chapter 9, "Posing Appropriate Questions"). Some of these issues may have been addressed earlier in the
interview, either because the topic arose naturally (e.g., the interviewer inquired about the child's experience in different households, thus eliciting information about discipline and the impact of
parental divorce) or because the child broached the subject. Some
children are more comfortable discussing topics such as domestic violence and pet abuse and may even "test" the interviewer's

responses to these disclosures before revealing their personal abuse history. Topics addressed in the closing section would be those the interviewer deems relevant but that have not been covered earlier in the interview.

C. Acknowledgment and Validation of the Child's Feelings

Some children will be feeling frightened or guilty regarding their disclosures. Some interviewers feel that it is important to address these issues during the interview, by asking children about their worries or fears and giving them the opportunity to discuss these feelings. These conversations are particularly justified when a child is obviously very upset or there is a risk of suicide. Some interviewers feel that this is not an appropriate role for the interviewer, because it removes the interviewer from a neutral stance. When the child's feelings are acute, it is recommended that at a minimum, the interviewer acknowledge the feeling and make an immediate referral to a therapist or a victim's advocate, if there is such a person onsite ("I can see that you are feeling upset. I'd like to bring in my friend, ___, who is a victim's advocate, so she can talk to you until you feel better"). When no onsite support is available, the interviewer should consider briefly discussing the issues with the child and making an immediate referral to a crisis center if necessary. See the "Cautionary Note" in this chapter for a discussion of related issues.

D. What Will Happen Next

With children school-aged and older, it may be helpful to talk with the child about what the future might hold and who may talk with the child in the future. For example, "I'm going to tell your mother I think you should have a talking person. Someone you could talk to about your feelings. If there is anything that you forgot to tell me today, you can tell your talking person. Sometimes the police might want to know, too, so they might come talk to you." Of course, if the interviewer chooses to address these issues, the conversation should vary according to the child's willingness to speak with counselors or police. This conversation should also vary according to center policy regarding reinterviewing children when new allegations surface.

E. Discussing the Child's Wishes or Desires

Some interviewers find it effective to ask children what they want to happen with their family or the perpetrator. Children may be asked "If you had three wishes, what would you wish for?" or "If you could change one thing about your family, what would that be?" These questions often provide helpful information regarding the child's affective state, family dynamics, and attachments to the perpetrator or other family members. This information is often helpful to the interviewer in making treatment recommendations and may be a good transition to therapy for some children. Other interviewers feel that these issues are best addressed in the therapeutic context, to maintain the neutrality of the child interviewer. Both positions are considered acceptable at the present time.

❏ *Practice Tip* ❏

Treats

As mentioned in Chapter 6, "Friendly, Neutral Approach to Children," snacks given noncontingently at the beginning of the interview are perfectly acceptable, even recommended. If the child is to be given any type of treat (stickers, stuffed animal) at the conclusion of the interview, it should be emphasized to the child that "every child who comes here gets one of these, no matter what happens." If possible, the fact that a treat will be given should not be mentioned until the end of the evaluation, to avoid the child becoming focused on the treat or perceiving a need to please the evaluators in order to receive a treat. In some cases, the interviewer may need to be quite direct regarding the lack of connection between the treat and the contents of the child's statements, especially if the child sees another child with a treat and is asking about it before the evaluation is concluded (e.g., "No matter what we talk about or don't talk about, every child who comes here gets a treat.

a treat. You will get one a little later. If I forget, you can remind me"). The interviewer may want to give the child a treat at the beginning of the evaluation, as a "snuggly," and to avoid the issue of perceived contingency.

❏ Cautionary Note

ON THE USE OF REASSURANCE

Some interviewers feel that it is important to reassure children that the abuse is not their fault or that they did the right thing to tell. In general, these tactics are discouraged because they compromise the interviewer's neutrality. Moreover, such techniques are important components of treatment, and treatment providers are likely to be more effective in conveying the message because they will be able to explore any resistance the child experiences to believing these reassurances (as when the affection felt good and the child sought it out, or when the perpetrator involved the child in a dysfunctional belief system).

It is important to note, however, that in some cases, a child may be very distraught, or guilty, and the interviewer may feel worried about the child's emotional well-being. At such times, compromises to the neutral stance may be justified in terms of protecting the child's mental health. If reassuring statements are used, the interviewer must be prepared to defend the departure from the neutral stance in court.

14

Verbatim Documentation

❏ Guideline

The interviewer should provide verbatim documentation of the interview, including the child's nonverbal behavior and affect.

❏ Supporting Information

1. DOCUMENTATION SHOULD INCLUDE THE INTERVIEWER'S QUESTIONS AND THE CHILD'S RESPONSES

It is important to document specific questions and answers, especially when the child is addressing who, what, when, and where information. The verbatim recording of the questions and answers provides the reader with a comprehensive overview of information disclosed. Documenting specific questions also provides the reader with the tools to evaluate the interview (e.g., Was it leading? Was it sensitive to the child's emotional needs? etc.).

2. A DESCRIPTION OF THE CHILD'S NONVERBAL
   BEHAVIORS PROVIDES A MORE PRECISE PRESENTATION
   OF THE INTERVIEW CONTENT

Utilizing descriptive words for body movements ("the child looked down, and her shoulders were slumped"), expressions ("she became teary-eyed"), positioning, and so forth, conveys to the reader the child's current affect, general adjustment, and response to the stress of the interview. Describing the nonverbal behavior during a child's disclosure underscores the impact of the child's statements on the interviewer and may convey information regarding the impact of the abuse on the child. Descriptions of nonverbal responses should also include statements regarding the child's responses to and manipulation of any tools used during the interview (e.g., anatomical dolls, drawings, etc.).

3. VERBATIM DOCUMENTATION MAY SUPPORT
   THE INTERVIEWER'S CREDIBILITY

Verbatim documentation is also a positive tool for the interviewer, who is frequently asked to appear in court to repeat statements made by the child. With the use of verbatim documentation, there is less room for supposition or interpretation on the part of persons evaluating the interview. In addition, the child may disclose details that are not useful to the investigation but that may be useful to other professionals involved with the child (e.g., child protection workers, treatment providers).

4. VERBATIM DOCUMENTATION MAY HELP THE
   CHILD BY DECREASING COURT APPEARANCES
   AND/OR REPEATED INTERVIEWS

Appearing in court is stressful for many children (see Goodman & Bottoms, 1993, for reviews). Verbatim documentation, particularly if it is in the form of an audio or video recording, may be presented to the court in lieu of the child for purposes of grand jury evaluations and even criminal trials. In addition, deposition time may be reduced if attorneys have access to recorded statements.

When an interview is thorough and includes the active input of officials from different disciplines, complete documentation should reduce the number of times a child has to repeat his or her statements. Reduction in the number of interviewers minimizes sources of contamination and is likely less stressful to the child.

5. THERE ARE SEVERAL RECORDING OPTIONS, INCLUDING VIDEOTAPING, AUDIOTAPING, AND NOTE-TAKING

Videotaping

There are many advantages to videotaping, which are listed here:

1. Children are spared multiple interviews (and interviewers).
2. The child's entire presentation (verbal and nonverbal) is preserved.
3. The camera provides a strong incentive for careful interviewing.
4. The tape wards off pressure to recant.
5. Interviews can be used in treatment to help parents acknowledge abuse.
6. Tapes are sometimes helpful in obtaining perpetrator confessions.
7. Attorneys can assess the strength of the witness without further questioning.
8. Video may appear in court in lieu of the child in some settings.
9. It preserves the earliest report, which is more reliable than testimony given months later   for example, in court.

It is also important to note possible disadvantages of videotaping. Child interviewers and assessment centers must establish carefully written policies to ensure that tapes are not obtained by persons with no regard for child confidentiality (e.g., news media). For some children, the taping process may make it more difficult to disclose. The interviewer must remain sensitive to this possibility and, when the issue arises, should offer the child choices to reduce the sense of scrutiny (e.g., hiding under the counter, whispering answers, writing answers). If these measures are not sufficient to reassure the child, the inter-

> *For some children, the videotaping process may make it more difficult to disclose.*

viewer should consult with the multidisciplinary team regarding suspension of the taping process. At times, a child will agree to audiotaping, and observers of the interview can help document the interview with written notes.

Audiotaping

With a few exceptions, audiotaping is associated with many of the same benefits as videotaping. However, audiotaping does not capture the nonverbal presentations of the child or the interviewer. At times, children respond nonverbally to questions (e.g., head nods, pointing, and using tools), and interviewer nonverbal behavior may provide clues regarding interviewer biases. Nonetheless, audiotaping is an excellent choice for field interviewing situations and when video is unavailable or not workable for a particular child. When a carefully written record is maintained along with audiotapes, some nonverbal behavior can be captured. Note-taking is an important adjunct to audiotaping.

Note-Taking

In many circumstances, note-taking is useful even if other recording options are used. In field situations, interviews are often conducted by teams of child protection workers and law enforcement. In these situations, one person can do most of the questioning, while the other carefully documents questions and answers. This format also is useful during medical exams. What follows is a list of advantages to note-taking:

1. The child may feel validated by seeing statements in writing.
2. The child can be included in correcting and confirming noted info.
3. Dictation time may be reduced for the interviewer (using notes versus tape).
4. The child is given time to reflect.
5. Interviewer attention is diverted, which gives emotional distance to the child.

Although there are many advantages to taking notes during an interview, there are times when note-taking is ill-advised. When a single individual is attempting to pose questions, and note both questions and the child's response, much of the child's nonverbal behavior may be missed, and the child may feel ignored while the interviewer is preoccupied with writing. This disadvantage is mostly overcome when interviewers work in teams, as noted earlier, or when note-taking is an adjunct to audio or video recording. At times, note-taking will be very difficult to accomplish, as with an active or distractible child or a child who needs a great deal of emotional support during the interview. Some centers advocate the simultaneous use of multiple recording procedures such as audio- or videotaping and note-taking, with the note-taking being abandoned at the interviewer's discretion during difficult interviews.

When note-taking is used as the primary documentation strategy, the original interview notes should be maintained in the agency's file. In addition, the county multidisciplinary team should establish policies regarding (a) who is responsible for generating reports from the notes, and (b) whether a single official report is generated or a mechanism exists for avoiding inconsistencies across multiple reports (Sorenson et al., 1997). When a single official report is generated, it may be helpful to have it reviewed for accuracy by each of the observers before a final report is generated.

❏   *Practice Tips*   ❏

1. Always introduce your documentation tools to the child

For example:

I: "Do you see the camera up there on the wall?"
C: (Nods affirmatively.)
I: "It takes down all of our words and makes pictures of us while we're talking. I use that to make sure I remember what we talked about today."

or

I: "I use this paper and pen to write things down while we
talk so I can be sure I remember what we talk about. It's
OK with me if you look at what I'm writing, and if I write
something wrong, you can tell me."

2. Recording equipment should be as unobtrusive as possible

Ideally, to reduce the possibility of reactivity (intimidation,
silliness), recording equipment would be located behind a
one-way mirror or a screen. If this is not possible, it should be
located high on a wall, so that it is not accessible to the child.

3. Use of video, audio, and written records is at the discretion of individual programs

The political and legal environments in which different programs operate must be considered in selecting a recording
option. In addition, the experience base within the local professional community may impact receptivity to some of these
options.

4. Training is essential for all staff operating audio or video equipment

It is helpful to minimize the number of staff operating the
recording equipment. These staff should be well-trained regarding the components of the equipment and their purposes,
as well as the purposes of and optimum settings for any dials
or buttons. Posting instructions for equipment use and trou-
bleshooting guides next to the equipment is a helpful adjunct
to training. It is also helpful to have signs instructing observers
not to touch the equipment and to contact the interviewer if
there is a concern that the equipment is malfunctioning during
an interview.

5. It is useful to have a back-up plan for audio or video recording

Equipment malfunctions invariably occur, sometimes ren-
dering the tapes unintelligible. At times, the interviewer is
unaware that the equipment is malfunctioning during taping.
The back-up plan may include the creation of multiple tapes
and/or note-taking during taping.

6. When notetaking is the primary recording option, teamwork is recommended

If notetaking is the only means of recording an interview, interviewers can work in teams, with two parties present during the interview (one can be behind a one-way mirror). One interviewer is "active" and initiates all questions, while the other functions as the "recorder," noting content, nonverbal reactions, and additional questions to ask (Yuille et al., 1993). The interview protocol could include a break, during which both interviewers decide final questions and compare notes regarding child demeanor.

7. Protective orders from a judge protect the child's confidentiality

When the child's records are involved in a court proceeding, the records become subject to public access, including the news media. Because the child has entrusted the interviewer with sensitive information, it is advisable for centers to take steps to prevent the tapes from being accessed by the general public. Centers can establish a policy that they do not release tapes to lawyers or other legal representatives unless a judge issues a protective order. The protective order can stipulate that the tapes will be returned to the center at the completion of legal proceedings and that the tape will not become part of the public record. See Appendix D for an example of a child protective order.

❑ Cautionary Note

WITH AUDIO OR VIDEO RECORDING, BE AWARE OF
THE LAWS GOVERNING RELEASE OF RECORDS

In medical settings, complex laws govern parents' rights to access records and parent and child confidentiality. As a consequence, it is advisable to consult legal counsel regarding preventing access in cases in which the parent is also the perpetrator or is supportive of the perpetrator. It is possible to write a consent form wherein a parent agrees to an oral summary in lieu of accessing the recordings of the interview.

These laws may not pertain in centers that follow an advocacy model rather than a medical model. Because the laws governing medical records exist to protect patient's rights and to ensure confidentiality, centers following an advocacy model will need to develop their own strategies to ensure protection of the child and confidentiality of the tapes.

PART III

Specialty Issues

Memory and Suggestibility

❏ Guideline

Children perceive, remember, and report events differently than do adults. Fundamentally, the interviewer's task is to cue the child's memory without tainting the memory or adversely influencing the way it is reported.

❏ Supporting Information: Memory

1. MEMORY VERSUS SUGGESTIBILITY

Memory refers to three basic processes: acquisition, storage, and retrieval of information based on prior experiences. All three processes are refined with age (McGough, 1994). **Suggestibility** refers to the likelihood of changing the memories themselves or a person's report of the memories by exposing the person to biasing influences such as leading questions, inaccurate information, or a coercive interviewer.

2. ACQUISITION REFERS TO EXPERIENCES TAKEN IN AND SENT TO MEMORY CENTERS FOR STORAGE

The term **trace strength** is often used to describe the accuracy of the acquisition process. It is possible to acquire a memory only for aspects of an event that were the focus of attention. Children may attend to different aspects of an event than adults (e.g., the color of a person's socks and shoes versus the color of hair and eyes; children are less attentive to time than adults). Whereas even adults don't take in all components of an event (e.g., the sound of the air conditioner), children perceive fewer aspects of complex events than adults. Children also are less able than adults to recognize their own and others' feelings and intentions (Perry, 1992). For these reasons, young children often do not respond well to "Why" questions. Children's ability to order and interpret events gradually develops and is similar to that of adults by the age of 12. Thus, an adult may be seeking information the child never took in, due to developmental limitations.

3. MEMORY STORAGE REFERS TO THE ABILITY TO KEEP MEMORY INTACT AND ACCURATE

Memory **storage** improves with age. Storage problems are often referred to as **trace decay.** Numerous studies indicate that as time passes, the reports of both children and adults are less complete and less accurate (Baker-Ward, Gordon, Ornstein, Larus, & Clubb, 1993; Flin, Boon, Knox, & Bull, 1992; Poole & White, 1995; Warren & Lane, 1995). Unfortunately, children forget more quickly than adults, and the younger the child, the faster the rate of forgetting. Immediately after an event, adult and child error rates are similar (less than 10%). With nonabusive events, error rates for children have doubled over a 5-month period and almost tripled over a 2-year period, whereas those for adults remained constant. It is important to note that studies of traumatic memories and memories for repeated events are less consistent in showing disproportionate difficulties with child memory (Kail, 1990; Terr, 1988). Nonetheless, potential problems with trace decay in children underscore the importance of rapid scheduling and careful documentation of initial child interviews.

4. MEMORY MAY BE ACQUIRED AND STORED IN VERBAL OR NONVERBAL MODES

It has been hypothesized that two memory systems operate throughout life (Pillemer & White, 1989). One memory system is based on sensory impressions, emotions, and faces and probably develops in infancy (Kail, 1990). In early infancy, children are able to **recognize** familiar faces and smells, and in later infancy (6 to 12 months) they are able to **recall** connections between their actions and particular consequences (e.g., kicking the mobile makes it move).

Both adults and children may resort to a nonverbal memory system in the face of emotionally overwhelming experiences.

The second memory system is verbally mediated and develops throughout the life span. Children rely increasingly on verbal storage processes as they age, probably using primarily verbal strategies by the time they are 7 or 8. Adult memory is primarily verbal. Some evidence indicates that both adults and children may resort to the nonverbal system in the face of emotionally overwhelming experiences (van der Kolk, 1994).

If memory is stored nonverbally, it will be difficult to elicit a report of the memory, both because questions (verbal cues) may not call up the memory and because, if the memory is elicited, children may have difficulty using words to describe what they recall (van der Kolk, 1994). While remembering, children may reexperience the event on a nonverbal level (feeling the way they did when it happened, seeing what happened, etc.).

It is important to note that the hypothesis that some memories are stored nonverbally is quite controversial at the present time. There is research suggesting that verbal recall of traumatic events is sometimes difficult, though researchers disagree regarding the source of the difficulty. Some researchers hypothesize that the memory was never stored (Ceci & Bruck, 1995), whereas others suggest that the memory was stored in a different location and can be recalled with nonverbal cues (van der Kolk, 1994). It is important to note that there is currently no research establishing that nonverbal memories can be evoked using nonverbal cueing procedures such as props. The current implication of this research for child interviewing is that verbally oriented interviews may not provoke full recall for some children, particularly those who were traumatized during the touching.

5. MEMORY RETRIEVAL PROBLEMS ARE WHY CHILDREN
   SOMETIMES REQUIRE ADULT ASSISTANCE IN THE FORM
   OF MEMORY CUES (FOCUSED QUESTIONS, PROPS).

Memory retrieval problems occur because of inadequate cueing, or because of an incomplete memory search.

From Birth to the Age of 2 or 3, Children Store Information Primarily in Nonverbal Memory. As the child ages, some memories, and some components of all memories continue to be stored nonverbally. If a child stores a memory or memory fragment in a sensory center, but verbal cues (e.g., questions) as opposed to sensory cues (e.g., touch) are used to elicit recall, the child may not access the memory. This process explains why children might disclose touching during a genital exam or a bath, where the sight and/or touching of their own private parts cues the memory. The same children may not disclose 15 minutes later when fully clothed in an interview room.

The More Elaborate a Memory, the More Easily the Memory is Cued. Adult memories contain information about time, place, person, actions, emotions, and the order of events (Fivush, 1993; Perry, 1992). Many of these components are missing from young children's memories (especially emotions, time, and event ordering), because the ability to perceive these components develops with age. Initially, children's memories contain only person and action information, with most components present at the age of 5½ to 7 years, and all components present by teenage years. Each memory component is a potential cue. The fewer components in a memory, the more difficult it will be to cue the memory.

> *The fewer components in a memory, the more difficult it will be to cue the memory.*

Children Have a More Limited Base of Experience Than Most Adults. Adult memories are embedded in a network of memory based on a lifetime of accumulated experience. Each connection to other memories acts as a potential memory cue (e.g., someone says something, which reminds you of one memory, which in turn reminds you of another memory, etc.). Obviously, because children's memories are missing important components and because there are fewer connections to other memories, it will be more difficult to cue children's memory. In fact, it may only be possible to elicit a child's memory with one or two specific cues (e.g., the word *poke* versus the word *touch*).

The problems in cueing children's memories are compounded by the fact that children are less able than adults to use strategies to search and fully retrieve memories. Examples of retrieval strategies include imagery, context reinstatement (making a picture in their mind of where and when the event occurred), organization (grouping similar items, such as "all the people I live with"), and internal or external cues (e.g., emotions such as "all the times I felt scared and nervous," or a string around the finger). Adults spontaneously use these strategies to cue memory initially and to ensure they report all of the details of the memory. Children may need help from the interviewer to use retrieval strategies and to fully retrieve the memory. Acceptable forms of help may include focused questions, non-leading props, and instructions on how to search and fully retrieve memories, though, as noted earlier in the document, the utility of each of these strategies is currently the subject of heated debate.

6. RECOGNITION VERSUS RECALL

Recognition memory involves exposure to a cue (a word, a picture, an object) and being able to accurately report prior exposure to the same cue. An example of recognition memory is identification of a perpetrator from a photo line-up. Recall involves spontaneous production of a memory, with minimal cueing (e.g., asking the child to provide a verbal description of the perpetrator's appearance). In general, during child interviews, we are asking for recall memory, though as more specific questions and props are included, some responses may involve only recognition memory.

7. ALL QUESTIONS PROVIDE SOME LEVEL OF MEMORY CUE

Open or "general inquiry" questions provide a low level of cueing, whereas leading questions provide an unacceptably high level of cueing. Young children may need help from the interviewer in the form of focused questions and instruction in the use of retrieval strategies. Studies with school-age children instructed on the use of retrieval strategies (context reinstatement, external cueing) and encouraged to use these in relating events have yielded improvements in the amount of accurate information reported (Geiselman et al., 1993). The utility of teaching memory retrieval strategies to preschoolers is unclear.

> *Children may retrieve a memory accurately, and then report it inaccurately.*

It is important to note that children might retrieve a memory accurately and then report it inaccurately.

8. WHEN EVENTS ARE REPEATED, RECALL MAY IMPROVE

When the same, or a similar, sequence of events occurs repeatedly, "scripts" describing persons, places, and objects involved, what actions occur, and the order of events develop in memory (Price & Goodman, 1990). Scripted events include brushing teeth, getting ready for bed, and games. Abusive activities may also provoke script development. Children as young as 2½ to 3 years old cluster actions into events and develop skeletal scripts involving central actions. With age and experience, scripts are elaborated through addition of peripheral detail and order information. Children's verbal recall of scripted knowledge is outstanding, beginning at the age of 4 to 5. Children aged 5½ can use and verbally report scripted knowledge at a level comparable to adults. Scripted knowledge is more easily retrieved with open-ended prompts than single event knowledge, particularly in young children. When a child discloses repeated abuse, researchers recommend first asking the child to explain "how and where it usually happens" to elicit the child's script knowledge. The interviewer can then ask about deviations from the script in terms of location, events, and timing (e.g., "You said the touching usually happened in the bedroom. Were there times Dad touched you in other rooms?"). It is important to note that some children, particularly younger children, will not be able to describe deviations from the script, even with prompts from the interviewer (Lindsay, Gonzales, & Eso, 1995; Price & Goodman, 1990).

9. MEMORY REPORTS ARE USUALLY IMPERFECT

In a given interview, it is rare for all the facts about a particular event to be reported (Fivush, 1993). Moreover, memories fade over time, especially memories of peripheral detail. As memory fades, individuals are more susceptible to suggestive questioning, and memories of similar experiences may blend together. Thus, new detail that was not part of the original memory may be incorporated (Loftus, 1979). These processes occur for both children and adults. The processes of forgetting and trace modification may be less pronounced with repeated events and with salient, personally experienced events (Fivush, 1993).

❏ Supporting Information: Suggestibility

10. THERE ARE LIKELY TO BE INDIVIDUAL DIFFERENCES IN SUGGESTIBILITY

Some children and adults are less suggestible than others. Some contexts are more risky for child suggestibility than others (Clarke-Stewart et al., 1989). Even in very leading contexts, some children continue to make accurate reports (cf. Leichtman & Ceci, 1995). In considering whether a child's report is influenced by suggestibility, it is important to look for specific sources of error. It is not acceptable to assume that just because children are young, their reports are influenced by suggestion. Research indicates that young children report quite accurately when they have not been coached and when they are neutrally interviewed (Ceci & Bruck, 1993).

Interviewers should be alert for signs of suggestibility (e.g., always answering yes to a question, reporting events from an adult perspective) and should be prepared to rephrase questions or gently challenge a child when suggestibility is a concern.

Suggestibility is influenced by the strength of the memory, language comprehension, source monitoring abilities, and the social context of the interview. Each of these influences on suggestibility will be reviewed in upcoming sections.

11. CHILDREN FORGET FASTER AND ARE THEREFORE MORE SUSCEPTIBLE THAN ADULTS

Strong memory (e.g., trace strength) inoculates against suggestibility. When a strong memory is present, a person is less likely to accept another person's interpretation of events. This phenomenon has been found with children as well as adults (Bruck, Ceci, Francoeur, & Barr, 1995). When incorrect information is given to children immediately after an event, while their memory is still strong, they are much less likely to go along with the suggestion. Children's memory for mundane events fades more quickly than adults. As time passes, children make more spontaneous errors in free recall *and* are more susceptible to the influence of a biased interviewer (McGough, 1994; Perry, 1992). It should also be noted that much of what children relate in a neutral interview is accurate, even with long delays. Interviewers should make every effort to avoid bias and interviews should be scheduled as soon as possible after the initial disclosure.

Children's memory for especially salient or traumatic events is not well-researched, and it is not clear if these memories fade as quickly. The conservative response is to assume that they do and to schedule interviews as quickly as possible. Unfortunately, many times a report of abuse occurs long after the event, and the best that can be done is to schedule the interview as soon after the disclosure as possible.

12. CHILDREN'S REPORTS ARE STRONGLY INFLUENCED BY LANGUAGE CAPABILITIES

It is important to remember that when interviewing children, we are not eliciting a raw memory; rather, we are asking a question, and receiving a verbal report of the child's memory. Communication is impaired if (a) the child fails to understand the question, (b) the child is unable to formulate a reply to the question or (c) the interviewer is unable to understand the child's reply. Many times children may have a memory of an event, but the interviewer's prompts are not an adequate cue, or the child lacks the skills to communicate the memory in a way that an adult can comprehend. These communication failures are as much a function of language capabilities as they are of child memory. See Chapter 10, "The Use of Language in Child Interviews," for more details and suggestions for avoiding language snafus.

13. AT TIMES, CHILDREN HAVE DIFFICULTY DISTINGUISHING EXPERIENCED EVENTS FROM EVENTS THEY HEARD OR DREAMED ABOUT

The ability to discriminate how, where, or from whom a piece of information was learned is called **source monitoring.** Preschool children sometimes have difficulty remembering how they acquired information. Consequently, they may not be able to distinguish information they directly experienced from information they were told about (Bruck, Ceci, Francoeur, & Barr, 1995; Lindsay, Gonzales, & Eso, 1995). The more similar two pieces of information are, the more difficulty children will have distinguishing the source of a memory (as with things they visualized occurring versus things that really happened).

It is interesting to note that among both children and adults, **source monitoring difficulties are especially pronounced if one imagines doing something,** particularly if this imaginative process occurs repeatedly (Ceci, Huffman, Smith, & Loftus, 1994; Ceci,

Loftus, Leichtman, & Bruck, 1994). This problem is more pronounced for children than for adults, even among older children (8 to 9 years old). Some children and adults may express uncertainty regarding whether they dreamed about an event or whether it really occurred. These sorts of reports may be more likely when a therapist has misused guided imagery and when abuse occurs at night, while the child is sleeping.

It should be noted at this point that details of sexual activity are not likely to be within the range of experience of most preadolescent children. Unless children witness an extended period of adult sexual activity, are told in great detail how such activity occurs, or participate directly in such activity, they are unlikely to dream about sexual activity or make reports of detailed sexual activity on the basis of what others have told them. Research on nonabused children indicates that they have trouble providing detailed accounts of events they did not experience, even when they were explicitly coached to do so and were provided with verbal details of the event (Tate & Warren-Leubecker, 1989). It is not acceptable to assume that a child has merely dreamed about an event, unless one has concrete information regarding the child's exposure to information that may have spawned the dream (e.g., pornography). One must also question why a child would accuse a particular individual; for example, how did this particular person become the focus of a sexualized dream or memory?

When young children are able to distinguish sources on a perceptual level, they may nonetheless struggle to find words to communicate these ideas. This problem is particularly pronounced among preschoolers. School-age children are increasingly able to tell whether someone told them something, versus whether they were there and actually witnessed or heard an event occurring. However, even school-age children are less likely than adults to spontaneously report the source of their information.

The interviewer should consider inquiring about information sources, especially when there is a concern about coaching, inappropriate therapy techniques, and dreaming about abuse. As with questioning about other areas, it is recommended that interviewers begin with open questions, such as "How did you know (Mom hit

Dad, Dad touched Suzy)?" or "When did you first remember Bobby touched you?" Some children, particularly younger ones, may respond better to multiple choice questions, such as "Do you remember Dad touching you, or did someone tell you about it?" If children express concern that they may have been dreaming, questions such as "What made you think it was a dream?"; "Was there anything about it that seemed real?"; "When did you decide it was a dream/real?"; or "What happened to make you change your mind?" can be clarifying. Source monitoring questions are also helpful if a family has been discussing abuse of a sibling, neighbor, or relative, and the child discloses this abuse during the interview. For example, the interviewer might ask, "Did you see ___ getting touched or did someone tell you about it?" It is important to note that preschoolers may not be able to provide source information even with questioning, and that preschoolers may be very sensitive to the phrasing of the questions (Poole & Lindsay, 1995). Until research provides more guidance regarding source monitoring questions with preschoolers, interviewers will need to carefully weigh risks (that a child will fail to understand the question and will select a response randomly) and benefits in using source monitoring questions with very young children. For other suggestions regarding detecting the influence of coaching, see Chapter 16, "Errors in Children's Reports."

14. THE SOCIAL CONTEXT INFLUENCES CHILDREN'S EVENT REPORTS

Children make many assumptions about adults that are significant in the interviewing context (Ceci & Bruck, 1993). Children assume that adults ask meaningful questions, that they are honest, and that adults know more than children. Children are also taught to please adults and to avoid challenging and insulting them. If an adult implies knowledge of an event, and this knowledge disagrees with the child's memory, the child may report the adult version despite accurate memory. Children may also attempt to answer questions when they have no memory of the event, and they may try to provide answers that make the adult happy. These assumptions about adults are more pronounced with younger children but may still be present to some degree in children as old as 9 or 10. Children may read the adult's verbal and nonverbal cues in order to decide how to please the adult. The importance of avoiding leading questions and preconceived biases is underscored by knowledge of children's social assumptions in the interviewing context. **The adult must make every effort to show interest in all of the child's statements. It is also helpful for adults to emphasize their ignorance of the events in question and the value placed on only knowing the truth about what happened.** See Chapter 8, "Setting the Stage," for details on introducing the child to the interview situation.

It is also worth mentioning that several research studies have examined the ability of children to implicate a person who is present during the interview. When a perpetrator is present during the interview, and especially if that person has admonished the child not to tell, the child is very unlikely to report on the perpetrator's actions (Batterman-Faunce & Goodman, 1993). These findings **emphasize the importance of interviewing the child alone and attempting to ensure that potential perpetrators do not accompany the child to the evaluation.**

Several studies have examined the effects of stress during acquisition on children's recall. Some studies suggest that stress improves recall, whereas others suggest that stress is detrimental to recall (Batterman-Faunce & Goodman, 1993; Peters, 1991). At the present time, the reasons for discrepant findings are unclear. Most studies indicate that stress during the interview impairs recall. **It is therefore important to interview the child in a low stress environment, whenever possible.** See the guidelines in Chapter 4, "Establishing a Neutral Environment," and Chapter 6, "Friendly, Neutral Approach to Children," for more details.

15. THREE QUESTIONS ABOUT SUGGESTIBILITY ARE OF PRIMARY INTEREST TO CHILD INTERVIEWERS

- How easy is it for an interviewer to provoke a false report?
- To what extent can children be encouraged by a significant other to make a false report or a false recantation?
- Can interviewers detect the influence of biases, coaching, or false reports?

16. INTERVIEWERS ARE UNLIKELY TO PROVOKE A
    FALSE REPORT WITH A SINGLE LEADING QUESTION

Several studies have carefully examined this issue (Leichtman & Ceci, 1995; Price & Goodman, 1990; Rudy & Goodman, 1991; Saywitz et al., 1991; Tobey & Goodman, 1992). Children have experienced physical examinations involving genital versus other touch and touching versus non-touching games with a "babysitter." When questioned with open questions and doll demonstrations of these events, the rate of false abuse reports was zero. With direct and misleading questions ("Did the man take his clothes off?"; "How many times did he spank you?") the false report rate ranged from 0% to almost 10%. Younger children (ages 4 or 5) and children who watched rather than directly experienced an event made higher rates of false reports. To be counted as a false report, the child merely had to assent to a leading question. Rates of false reports with convincing detail were much lower—0% to 3%.

Stephen Ceci and colleagues (Bruck, Ceci, Francouer, & Barr, 1995) acknowledge these findings, stating, **"Children rarely make false claims about touching, and particularly about sexual touching, in response to a single misleading question in a single interview."**

The foregoing information underscores the need to evaluate the interview in toto, rather than on a question-by-question basis. A single mistake is unlikely to forever taint a child's memory. Interviewers should nonetheless be careful in how they question children, as multiple, biased interviews with many leading questions can provoke significant rates of false reports (cf. Leichtman & Ceci, 1995). See the guidelines in Chapter 9, "Posing Appropriate Questions" and Chapter 16, "Errors in Children's Reports," for more details regarding questioning children.

17. WITH VERY BIASED INTERVIEWS, SOME
    CHILDREN MAKE FALSE REPORTS

The definitions of biased interviews versus neutral interviews originally noted in Chapter 5, "Single Versus Multiple Interviewers," will be repeated here, to clarify distinctions between them and to assist the reader in interpreting relevant research. Biased interviews are those in which the interviewer attempts to guide the child into making particular statements that confirm the interviewer's hypotheses about what happened to the child. Biased interviews typically will include one or more of the following components: asking numerous leading questions ("Your dad touched your privates, didn't he?"), making coercive statements ("You'll feel better once you tell," "I know something bad happened to you, don't be afraid to tell me"), making pejorative comments about the alleged perpetrator (e.g., "Bill is bad," "Bill does bad things," "Your friends told me what Bill did to them"), and/or providing supportive comments only when the child discloses abuse (see Ceci & Bruck, 1995, for a review). Neutral interviews (Ceci & Bruck, 1995) are characterized by limited numbers of leading or suggestive questions, a lack of motive for the child to make a false report, and a neutral stance by the interviewer (e.g., no coercion, acceptance of the child's statements without undue positive or negative emotion; see Chapter 6, "Friendly, Neutral Approach to Children," for more information).

Aside from the impact of asking leading questions (which was thoroughly reviewed in Chapter 9, "Posing Appropriate Questions"), two mechanisms for influencing a child's statements have been studied. One involves repeatedly providing a child biased information before or after an event occurs ("Sam is a clumsy person"; "He wasn't supposed to do that"; "That was bad"), and the other involves repeated direct and misleading questions after an event. The combined influence of these approaches has also been studied (Clarke-Stewart et al., 1989; Leichtman & Ceci, 1995; Lepore & Sesco, 1994).

When children are encouraged to develop a stereotype or bias against a person and/or are repeatedly given postevent misinformation, high error rates may result. In Lepore and Sesco's (1994) study, 4- to 6-year-old children played with a man named "Dale." Later, some of these children described what happened with Dale, and the interviewer interpreted the child's statements in a negative light, for example, "Dale wasn't supposed to do that. That was bad." Of these children, 33% made false accusations about Dale that were embellished with peripheral detail. When 5- to 6-year-old children were led to believe Sam Stone was a clumsy person before they met him (the biased group), 20% made false reports in response to direct questions (Leichtman & Ceci, 1995). When unbiased 5- to 6-year-old children were repeatedly asked questions about things that never happened with Sam Stone, the rate of false accusations rose to 40%. Combining biases and repeated misleading questions did not raise the error rate; that is, for 5- to 6-year-old children with both types of influence, the error rate remained at about 40% (Leichtman & Ceci, 1995). When children were interrogated by a biased interviewer and actively persuaded to adopt the interviewer's interpretation of the events, rates of false reports ranged from 90% after a single, long interview to almost 100% after two interviews (Clarke-Stewart et al., 1989).

Error rates for young children (3- to 4-year-olds) in the Sam Stone study were higher, almost 40% with biases alone, 35% to 50% with repeated direct and misleading questions, and up to an astonishing 72% when both influences were present (Leichtman & Ceci, 1995).

It is important to note that this research applies only to the worst examples of child interviewing, and the types of mistakes made by these interviewers can easily be avoided. See the guidelines in Chapter 5, "Single Versus Multiple Interviewers," Chapter 9, "Posing Appropriate Questions," and Chapter 11, "The Use of Repeated Questions in Interviews" for specific suggestions. It is also important to note that these interviewers did not ask abuse questions involving the child's own body (e.g., "Did Sam touch your private parts?" or "Did Chester spank you?"). Based on previous studies, rates of false accusations to these types of questions are likely to be quite a bit lower. Finally, it is important to note that these studies typically included small numbers of nonabused, white, middle-class children. More research on larger and more diverse samples is needed before firm conclusions can be drawn regarding the potential influence of biased interviews on children's accounts of abuse.

18. WHEN CHILDREN ARE COACHED OR UNINTENTIONALLY MISLED BY PARENTS

The sources of biased information and misleading questions in the previous studies were nonfamilial adults. A couple of studies have examined rates of erroneous reports with parental coaching. In Poole and Lindsay's (1995) study, parents read a story containing both accurate and inaccurate information about the child's earlier interaction with "Mr. Science." Children aged 3 to 4 were interviewed twice, once immediately after they interacted with Mr. Science and once three months later, shortly after the partially erroneous stories had been read. The children were highly accurate in the initial interviews but highly inaccurate when incorrect information was supplied by their parents (41% made errors in free recall, 53% falsely accused Mr. Science of putting something yucky in their mouths, and 88% falsely reported the occurrence of at least one event in response to many leading questions). In studies in which parents have intentionally coached a child to provide a false report, error rates have been even higher (Devitt et al., 1994). These studies underscore the importance of inquiring about previous conversations familial and nonfamilial adults have had with the child. It is helpful to ask both the parents and the child about these issues (e.g., for the parent: "What first made you concerned that your daughter had been abused?"; "How did you react when you found out?"; "Did your child see/hear your reaction?"; "Did you talk to your daughter about what happened?"; "I know it's hard to remember, but can you try to tell me exactly what questions you asked, and how she responded?"). See Chapter 16, "Errors in Children's Reports" and Section 20 of this chapter for suggestions on questioning the child regarding parental biases and coaching.

19. INDIVIDUAL DIFFERENCES IN SUSCEPTIBILITY TO BIASED INTERVIEWERS

Although the error rates in the previously cited "Sam Stone" and "Dale" studies were at times disturbingly high, it is important to note that a substantial proportion of children also resisted the biased interviewers and the leading questions. In the Sam Stone study, 80% of the 5- to 6-year-olds exposed to bias alone made accurate reports, as did 67% of the 4- to 6-year-old children in the Dale study. With leading questions and/or biases, 60% of the 5- to 6-year-old children continued to make accurate reports in the Sam Stone study. In summary, **the majority** of 5- to 6-year-old children continued to make accurate reports even in the context of very bad interviews. Similar results held with 3- to 4-year-olds, except those exposed to both biases and leading questions. **These re-sults underscore the notion that a child's report cannot be dismissed simply because of exposure to a single bad interview.** However, the emphasis on the fact that many children were accurate in these contexts does not imply that interviewers can relax their standards, because these high error rates are

> *A child's report cannot be dismissed simply because of exposure to a single bad interview.*

unacceptable in the forensic context, where false reports may have serious consequences. It is also important to recall that particularly long coercive interviews and/or repeated bad interviews may provoke higher error rates, as might interactions with biased parents (see Clarke-Stewart et al.'s 90% to 100% error rates and Poole & Lindsay's 41% to 88% error rates).

20. QUESTIONING CAN BE HELPFUL IN DETECTING THE INFLUENCE OF BIASES AND COACHING

In the previously mentioned "Sam Stone" study, false reports were gently challenged, for example, "Did you see Sam rip the book?" and "Are you sure you saw Sam rip the book?" With challenges, rates of false reporting dropped dramatically (i.e., from 72% to 21% among 3- to 4-year olds who had been biased and misled, and from 38% to 8% among a similar group of 5- to 6-year olds). This research implies that **when an interviewer is concerned about a false report, gently challenging questions (e.g., "Are you sure. . . ?"; "Was anything you told me pretend or not true?") may be helpful.** Other more general questions about direct experiences and sensory experiences may also be helpful, for example, "How did you know about ___?"; "Were you there when it happened, or did someone tell you about it?"; "What did you see/feel/taste/touch while ___ (Daddy poked your potty)?" or "Where were you when ___ (Mommy hit Daddy)?" All such questions should be posed with neutral affect.

In situations in which the child's report has changed **significantly** and there is a concern regarding coaching in the family, at the end of the interview questions exploring the source of the discrepancy can be posed. For example, "Today you told me ____. Did you ever tell someone else that it happened a different way?" If the child admits to having told someone else a different version, the interviewer can explore the reason(s) the child's report changed (e.g., "How come you told Officer Tim ___ and me ____? Did someone talk to you? Did something happen to change your mind?"). Children can also be asked if someone else has told them a different version of events or asked them to keep secrets or lie about the events (e.g., "Did someone else talk to you about the touching?"; "What did Mom say about the touching?"; "What did your dad do/say when you told him about the touching?"; "Was there anything your dad wanted you to tell me today?"; "Will anyone be mad if you tell the truth today?"). **It is critical to note that these sorts of challenges should be reserved for major discrepancies (e.g., changes in the name of the alleged perpetrator, denying abuse in one interview versus admitting extensive abuse in another) and for contexts in which there is significant concern regarding attempts to influence the child's statements.** As noted earlier, inconsistencies and minor discrepancies are normal phenomena when children, particularly young ones, are interviewed multiple times by different people in different circumstances, because changes in interviewer style and circumstances may prompt recall of different memories or different aspects of the same memory. See Chapter 16, "Errors in Children's Reports," and Chapter 17, "The Nondisclosing Child," for more discussion of errors in children's reports.

In the absence of questions regarding coaching and biases, the interviewer and other professionals are unlikely to be capable of discriminating detailed false reports from accurate reports. In several studies, professionals with considerable experience in the field have been asked to evaluate children's unchallenged statements. These professionals performed no better than chance at discriminating true from false reports, when both types of reports were elaborate and the statements were unchallenged (Ceci et al., 1994; Leichtman & Ceci, 1995).

16

Errors in Children's Reports

There are five possible outcomes to a child abuse assessment:

- true disclosure,
- false disclosure,
- true denial/recantation,
- false denial/recantation, and
- unable to determine.

True disclosure and true denial or recantation are desired outcomes of the assessment. The upcoming sections deal with concerns regarding false disclosures and false denials or recantations. At times, false reports will occur due to language problems or memory problems. These issues are addressed in "The Use of Language in Child Interviews" and "Memory and Suggestibility" chapter guidelines.

❏ **Guideline**

When an interviewer or other multidisciplinary team member is
concerned that a child is making a false report, the interviewer should
ask clarifying questions, so long as the questioning process will not
be unduly stressful to the child.

❏ **Supporting Information**

1. FALSE REPORTS ARE RARE

The actual incidence of false reports is difficult to establish, due
to the unavailability of well-validated indicators of a statement's
truth versus falsehood. Studies of nonabused populations aged 4
and older, in which a child is exposed to a known event (e.g., a
genital versus a scoliosis exam), estimate that rates of false accusations of touching range from 1% with direct but non-leading questions (Saywitz, Goodman, Nicholas, & Moan, 1991) to 30% or more
with leading questions over a number of sessions (see Ceci & Bruck,
1995, for a review). In samples of abused children in which some
knowledge of the events is available (polygraphs, perpetrator con-
fession) or experts judge child believability, estimates of false reporting range from 1% to 10% (Faller, 1996b). The incidence of false
reports is believed to be somewhat higher in samples in which
families are engaged in custody battles (14%; Faller, 1990b; Thoennes & Tjaden, 1990), or when the child is an adolescent with a motive
to fabricate (8%; Everson & Boat, 1989).

2. POSSIBLE SOURCES OF CHILDREN'S FALSE REPORTS

False reports can be intentional or unintentional. In some cases,
children may dislike the perpetrator and may lie about misdeeds in
order to achieve particular outcomes (ending their mother's violent
relationship with the perpetrator). Parents may also intentionally
coach a child to alter their entire report or significant parts of the

report (e.g., "You can talk about what happened with Uncle Bobby, but don't tell about Dad"; "If the doctor asks about your bruises, say you fell"). It is very difficult to know which children will comply with parental requests to lie and under what conditions. For example, some evidence suggests that 3- to 4-year-olds have a difficult time maintaining a lie, whereas 5- to 7-year-old children can and will maintain a lie (Bussey, Lee, & Grimbeek, 1993; Devitt et al., 1994). Other evidence suggests that children 3 to 7 years old are difficult to coach into lying and that their false reports are less detailed than those of children who actually experienced the event (Tate, Warren, & Hess, 1992). There is a widespread belief that emphasizing the importance of telling the truth and gently challenging the child's statements will cause many children to relinquish a lie. This possibility has not been well-researched, though clinical experience suggests that these techniques are effective with some children.

In other cases, it is likely that an adult did not directly coach a child's statements but rather communicated a bias to the child. The adult's bias may have been incorporated into the child's memory or may have predisposed the child to misinterpret benign events (as when a child interprets her father tucking her into bed as attempted suffocation). Research supports the influence of bias on perception. Children told by an adult that a visitor is clumsy or abusive adjust their reports of the visitor's behavior in line with the adult's biases (Clarke-Stewart et al., 1989; Leichtman & Ceci, 1995). These influences on children's reports may be particularly pernicious. With repeated biased interactions or when children imagine things that never happened, the children may come to believe that the events occurred. In these cases, the child is not lying but may make a false report on the basis of a false belief about what happened. At times, these false reports may be indistinguishable from true reports (Ceci, Huffman, Smith, & Loftus, 1994; Ceci, Loftus, Leichtman, & Bruck, 1994). As noted in the previous chapter, research evidence suggests that nonfamilial interviewers must commit egregious errors to produce this sort of false report. On the other hand, coaching and biasing by a parent may be particularly effective in altering a child's report (Devitt et al. ,1994; Poole & Lindsay, 1995). It is important to note that these studies have not examined children's willingness to go along with suggestions of abusive touch. Firm conclusions regarding the influences of adult biases on children's perceptions and reports in the context of an interview regarding possible abuse await further research.

3. THE DEVELOPMENT OF LYING IN CHILDREN

The act of lying involves several cognitive skills: discerning the truth; having awareness that another person can maintain a false belief; having a willingness to deceive; and having the ability to provide misinformation. Children as young as 4 are able to accurately discriminate between the truth and a lie using stories (Bussey, 1992; Lyon, 1996). Reports of parent surveys indicate that 4-year-old children lie almost five times a week, typically to conceal misdeeds (Stouthamer-Loeber, 1987). Thus, children as young as 4 comprehend the difference between the truth and a lie and seem by their willingness to attempt lying to understand that another person can maintain a false belief.

> *When children anticipate punishment, they are more likely to lie.*

Regarding children's willingness to deceive, experimental studies indicate that when children anticipate punishment, they are more likely to lie (Lewis, Stanger, & Sullivan, 1989). At around the age of 5 or 6, the ability to anticipate consequences and to lie convincingly becomes more developed. However, at this same age, children begin to internalize societal norms, and their willingness to lie may decline (Bandura, 1991; Bussey, 1992).

Children's ability to lie varies according to the level of detail necessary. Experimental studies indicate that it is easier for a child to lie by saying "no" than by having to memorize a concocted story and tell it convincingly (Tate, Warren, & Hess, 1992). This is particularly true for younger children. When reports of children coached to falsely report playing with a toy were compared with children who actually played with the toy, children making false reports provided less detail. Older children provided more detail than younger children. Thus, it is important for the interviewer to explore and document details of the child's report.

Studies have not yet addressed a child's ability/willingness to alter single details of otherwise true events when coached (e.g., "He wasn't washing your privates, he was poking his finger inside").

4. INCONSISTENCIES DO NOT NECESSARILY MEAN A CHILD IS MAKING A FALSE REPORT

Many individuals, including those involved in the criminal justice system, believe that when a child reports different things in different interviews, the child is lying (Ross, Miller, & Moran, 1987). In several studies, children have been shown to be highly accurate (90% accurate) in reporting events but to report very different aspects of the event in different interviews (Fivush, 1993). Accuracy and consistency are not highly correlated. Thus, it is normal for children to give different details to different interviewers and to the same interviewer at different times. See Chapter 5, "Single Versus Multiple Interviewers," and Chapter 10, "The Use of Language in Child Interviews," for more detail.

What follows are some explanations for inconsistencies in children's reports both within and across interviews. When possible, given the child's age and circumstances, the evaluator should probe for sources of inconsistencies and should rule out the following explanations before concluding that a child is making a false report:

- The child is telling you about different incidents.
- The child is discussing different aspects of the same incident.
- The current interviewer or a previous interviewer misinterpreted the child's statements.
- The child doesn't comprehend the interviewer's language, and responds to multiple choice or yes/no questions at random.
- The child acquiesced to leading questions during this interview or during a prior interview.
- The child may have been fearful or unwilling to speak openly with one of the interviewers.

5. HANDLING INCONSISTENCIES:
   RULING OUT LANGUAGE

The most important methods of handling inconsistencies are to prevent language-based difficulties by asking simple questions, assessing the child's comprehension of important forensic concepts, and avoiding leading questions (see Chapters 9 and 10, "Setting the Stage" and "The Use of Language in Child Interviews," for more detail).

When a child's report has been elicited using multiple choice and yes/no questions (as with a very young or very frightened child), the interviewer should be alert regarding possible response biases such as recency (choosing the last alternative) and acquiescence (always choosing yes). To test for the presence of these biases, the interviewer may want to re-ask one or two questions with the alternatives in a different order. With multiple choice questions, the recency bias can also be avoided by always making the final alternative an open-ended one (e.g., ". . . or some other room"; ". . . or something else"). To test for the aquiescence response bias, the question should be rephrased so that a yes response implies a different answer. For example:

1. Initial question: "Did it feel bad?"
   Follow-up question: "Did it feel good?"
2. Initial question: "Did he touch with his hand?"
   Follow-up question: "Did he touch with his foot?"

6. HANDLING INCONSISTENCIES:
   RULING OUT MULTIPLE INCIDENTS

Once language-based difficulties are ruled out as explanations for inconsistent details, the interviewer should explore whether the child is describing different incidents or different aspects of the same incident. Asking questions to elicit peripheral detail (e.g., "Where" and "When" questions) can be very helpful in this regard. For example, if the child has stated that clothes were on at one point in

"You said your clothes were on when he touched you. Where were you when your clothes were on? When did that happen? What kind of touching happened with clothes on? When we talked about kissing, you said your clothes were off. Where were you when that happened? When did that happen? How did your clothes get off?"

> *It is sometimes helpful to encourage a running narrative.*

It is also helpful to encourage a running narrative. In the previous example, if the child said the events all happened on the same day, in the same place, the interviewer could say:

"You've told me about several things that happened: touching, kissing, clothes off, but I'm having trouble putting it all together. Can you tell me what happened first? Then what? (and so forth)."

7. EXAMINING ABILITY AND MOTIVATION TO MAKE A FALSE REPORT: THE SOCIAL HISTORY

The most important components of the social history in this regard are sources of sexual knowledge and observations of the nonoffending caretakers. The child's prior abuse history, experience in witnessing parents' or other adults' sexual activity, and viewing pornography are important to assess. A child with no prior knowledge of sexual activity is unlikely to be capable of producing a convincing fabrication.

The child's ability to provide detail discriminating between incidents is important in sorting out the impact of prior abuse. The presence, quality of, and verifiability of peripheral detail are important in discriminating reports based on direct versus vicarious experience (e.g., being touched versus witnessing parents' sexual activity, overhearing parents' conversations regarding the alleged perpetrator's actions, or viewing pornography).

Observations of nonoffending caretakers can provide important clues to the child's social milieu and potential sources of bias. Asking the caretakers about their history with the perpetrator, their reactions to the allegations, and their desired outcomes (jail, family reunification) provides context to evaluate potential false state-reactions to the allegations, and their desired outcomes (jail, family reunification) provides context to evaluate potential false statements and false denials. Similar questions can be asked of a therapist, when there is a concern regarding bias or leading treatment approaches. It is important to note that in very complex cases, all of these details may not be gathered by the child interviewer due to time constraints (e.g., the child is becoming fatigued while waiting for the parent to be interviewed) and/or cost constraints on the interviewer's assessment. In these cases, law enforcement investigators can interview parents and therapists to follow up on any concerns regarding the influence of biased adults.

8. EXAMINING ABILITY AND MOTIVATION TO MAKE A FALSE REPORT: INTERVIEWING TECHNIQUES

Particularly when the social history prompts concerns regarding parental bias or coaching, children can be questioned regarding their perceptions of the situation. For example:

"How do you feel about (alleged perpetrator)?"

"How did you feel about (alleged perpetrator) when you first met him? What changed your mind about him?"

"Is there anything bad (or good) that might happen because you told?"

"What are you going to do after we're done talking?" I once spoke to a child who was going to have a "hero" party after her evaluation, if she disclosed.

"How does (biased person: Mom, therapist) feel about (alleged perpetrator)? How do you know that?"

"Have you told other people about the touching? Who? What did (biased person) say?"

"Did anyone (or use name of biased person) talk to you about coming to see me today? What did he/she say?"

"Is there anything you're supposed to tell me today? Who told you to tell me that?"

❑ **Cautionary Note**

CHALLENGING A CHILD'S STATEMENT

When all other explanations have been ruled out, the interviewer can consider challenging the child's statements. Please note that if contradictory information was obtained from a source other than the child, confrontation of the child should be carefully considered, because this approach is quite leading. If it is to be done, it should be done at the end of the interview, so as to minimize contamination of information obtained earlier in the interview. Even if it is done at the end of an interview, consideration should be given to the fact that it might contaminate future interviews, as well as court testimony. In addition, confrontation of the child with this type of information could produce an adverse emotional impact on the child. The child might feel disbelieved and/or "ganged up on." Such a confrontation could also undermine efforts to create an atmosphere of neutrality and acceptance, because confrontation of this sort is likely to be interpreted as a challenge. In other words, confrontation of a child with information obtained from other people should be a method of last resort, and the interviewer should be well aware of the compromises this procedure produces, both in rapport-building with the child and in the ability to interpret the child's statement.

When confrontation is considered, it is recommended that the interviewer remain congenial and supportive toward the child. The interviewer can say something like:

"I'm confused. First you told me ___, then you told me ___. Can you help me understand what really happened?" or "Can you tell me again so those two things make sense to me?"

17

The Nondisclosing Child

❏ Guideline

Nondisclosure is an acceptable and likely outcome to many child abuse interviews. There are many possible reasons for nondisclosure in a given interview. When there is a concern regarding barriers to disclosure, the interviewer must assess the child's ability to handle sensitive clarifying questions.

❏ Supporting Information

1. THE INCIDENCE OF NONDISCLOSURE IN CHILD ABUSE INTERVIEWS

Several studies have examined the rates of nondisclosure among children suspected of being abused who were referred for interviews. In initial interviews, 72% of Sorenson and Snow's (1991) sample of likely victims did not disclose, whereas over several interviews about 96% disclosed. In Lawson and Chaffin's (1992) sample of children with sexually transmitted diseases, 43% disclosed in an initial interview, although the disclosure rate among a subsample of children with an unsupportive parent dropped to 17%. Studies such as these underscore the interviewer's concern regarding barriers in cases of nondisclosure. Equally valid is the notion that misunderstandings do occur, and there are likely valid cases of nondisclosure even in heavily prescreened samples.

2. REASONS CHILDREN DO NOT DISCLOSE

There Is Nothing to Disclose

Particularly with young children, the child's statements or physical symptoms may have been misinterpreted. For example, a child returns from visits with her father displaying a red bottom, but the father uses bubble bath (which is irritating to the vagina); or a child makes a statement about a particular individual hurting her private, but this occurred during play (sand got in it) or during normal bathing and toileting. Parents may panic when confronted with these symptoms, and the child may lack the verbal skills to clarify and/or the parents do not ask appropriate clarifying questions.

The Child Is Afraid

The child may be afraid of being disbelieved, as when there is an unsupportive parent or extended family network. The perpetrator may have threatened the child directly (verbally) or indirectly (via harsh discipline or domestic violence toward other family members). Research shows that adult threats are particularly powerful incentives for nondisclosure in children (Bussey et al., 1993). If the touching was by a same-sex offender, the child may be worried about being homosexual or being labeled homosexual.

The Child Is Ambivalent

Many abusers are trusted family members and friends. The child may have disliked the touch but may also maintain positive memories with and loving feelings toward the offender. In addition, the child may be aware that the disclosure will be very disrupting to the family (financially, emotionally, and practically, if the child is forced to move and change schools).

The Child Is Ashamed

The child may be embarrassed saying the words or talking with a stranger regarding these issues. Similarly, the child may have experienced pleasurable feelings during the abuse and may not have even viewed it as abusive. Some children "buy into" the perpetrator's belief system regarding special time and showing love through touching. Children may also be concerned regarding their own culpability in seeking the affection with this abuser and/or sexually reactive behavior with other children.

The Memories May Not Be Accessible During This Conversation

With extremely high anxiety, or before language is developed, some events are never encoded or are nonverbally encoded so that they are less accessible and more difficult to recall using a conversational format (van der Kolk, 1994). Other children may be denying, suppressing (consciously deciding, "I will not think about this"), or repressing (unconsciously pushing away) their memories.

Children may deny, suppress, or repress their memories.

The Child May Have Trouble Relating to a Particular Interviewer

These responses may relate to inadequate rapport development or to the interviewer's style. At times, children may need more time to develop rapport than is available during a single interview. Some children may feel invaded by an overly warm interviewer, whereas other children may feel insecure with a more neutral interviewer. Other responses may be more idiosyncratic, for example, some children feel particularly uncomfortable with one gender, or the interviewer may remind the child of the perpetrator or a hated teacher.

The Setting Intimidates the Child

The presence of a particular observer (the police) or of observers in general (as with an early adolescent child) may be intimidating or distracting to the child. The child may also have an adverse reaction to the videotaping process, particularly if the equipment is obtrusive.

3. HELPING A CHILD VOLUNTEER INFORMATION (MORGAN, 1995)

The most important thing the interviewer can do is to help the child feel safe and comfortable in the interviewing context. The importance of adequate **rapport development** cannot be overemphasized. When children feel supported, they are more likely to answer honestly and volunteer information regarding an abuse allegation. Morgan (1995) suggests that inteviewers frequently remind the child of their role (someone who helps kids with problems) and that interviewers exhibit an understanding of children's problems. For example, interviewers can let the child know that they've talked to lots of other children with similar problems and can give the child examples of other problems children have discussed with them (abuse and nonabuse; e.g., hot peppers in the mouth, people hurting their feelings). These activities emphasize that the interviewer is someone children can trust.

Morgan (1995) has several suggestions for activities that are good rapport-builders and may help the child supply information regarding possible abuse. What follows is a summary of her suggestions, with some additions based on my clinical experience. It must be emphasized that these techniques extend discussion with the child, and the interviewer should be genuinely interested in all of the information the child provides. The information obtained is likely to be useful in the absence of disclosure, and it may provide the interviewer the opportunity to help the child with other (nonabuse) difficulties. The interviewer may also use the opportunity to do some prevention work.

Morgan suggests creating a **favorite/least favorite (or like/don't like) list,** wherein children will supply names, relationships, and other information regarding people they live with and/or visit (babysitters, grandparents, noncustodial parents). The interviewer probes regarding specific positive and negative feelings toward each of these individuals. This activity provides helpful information regarding the child's daily living environment and contextual information in case of an abuse disclosure.

Morgan also suggests a **problem-solving discussion** with the child. Interviewers begin by informing the child that their job is to help children and families who may have a problem, question, or concern. The interviewer then asks if there is any problem the child is having. If the child doesn't name any problems, the interviewer can discuss different levels of problems, such as those children can solve by themselves (their shoe comes untied, they want a different color crayon) versus those in which they might need help from a friend or family member (your brother took your toy) versus those in which they might want help from outside the family (someone stole your lunch at school, you broke your arm). Following this discussion, the interviewer would again query whether there is a problem the interviewer can help with.

The interviewer can also discuss **privacy** with the child. The interviewer can define *privacy* for younger children (Morgan suggests, "being able to be alone when you want to be") but may want to have older children attempt a definition. Subsequently, questions about when the child likes privacy, what rooms are good for privacy, and what the child likes to do in private can ensue. Morgan suggests that the interviewer ask about different people in the home and whether they are good or not so good at letting the child have privacy. The interviewer can also ask about whether there are things they do in private that they don't like or don't want to do.

Finally, Morgan suggests initiating a discussion of **safety rules.** The interviewer can discuss fire safety, bike safety, walking to and from school, and personal safety (encountering strangers, private parts). The interviewer should encourage the child to list safety rules for each topic. The child and interviewer can then discuss why these rules are important and whether there are times when it is difficult to follow the rules (e.g., your friends are riding their bikes across the intersection without looking). The interviewer can also ask about different people and how well they follow safety rules.

When a child is having a great deal of difficulty developing rapport, the interviewer may want to consider a multisession format, to provide the child with an opportunity for extended rapport development. Some of Morgan's activities could be part of a multisession format. It is important to note that if the interviewer is concerned that the child is not ready to disclose, a referral to treatment in a nondirective atmosphere may be more appropriate than multiple interviews. With older children, the interviewer may address this issue directly, asking children if they would like to come back for another interview or go directly into treatment.

> *When a child is having a great deal of difficulty developing rapport, consider a multisession format.*

4. DISCUSSIONS OF PET CARETAKING ROUTINES MAY HELP A CHILD DISCUSS PARALLEL ISSUES

Boat (1995) notes that there is evidence to suggest a link between the type of care provided to children and care provided to pets in the same household. Likewise, in many homes in which there is domestic violence or child abuse, the pets are also being abused. Dr. Boat recommends the following set of questions to assess pet caretaking:

Do you have any pets? What kinds of pets do you have?
Who takes care of the pets at your house?
What happens when the pets are naughty?
Have you ever lost a pet? What happened?
Have you ever worried about your pets / that bad things were happening to your pets?

These questions can be a useful bridge from rapport-building to discussions of abuse or neglect to the child and can help the interviewer detect the need for intervention from animal protection authorities as well. An interviewer's response to disclosures about pet safety can also help children feel safe discussing their personal abuse history.

5. WHEN IS NONDISCLOSURE A PROBLEM?

It cannot be emphasized enough that it is not the interviewer's job to elicit disclosure. The appropriate stance for the interviewer is that of a careful questioner striving to elicit reliable, factual statements regarding bodily touch and exposure to other risk factors. Consequently, it is perfectly appropriate for the interviewer to accept a child's nondisclosure, particularly if it is offered with neutral or positive affect and/or the child provides plausible explanations for prior statements (as when Daddy poked the pee pee accidentally during bathing or Mommy tickled the lower abdomen rather than the private part).

Under some circumstances, the interviewer may be concerned regarding the lack of disclosure. Such a situation may arise with very young children who have difficulty disclosing to strangers; when a child has an abnormal exam but is not disclosing; when a child lives in high risk circumstances and there has been familial pressure to recant; and when a child has disclosed extensively to other professionals but is denying during this interview.

6. UNACCEPTABLE TACTICS

Both research and clinical considerations advise against leading questions, repeated questioning, bribing the child (e.g., "We can keep you safe only if you tell"), or coercing the child ("You can't leave until you tell me what happened"). It would also be unacceptable for a field interviewer or parent to enter the interview room and encourage the child to repeat what was previously disclosed, because the child may have important reasons for deciding not to redisclose (fears of family breakup, threats, or a prior interviewer who misunderstood or used leading questions/coercion to elicit the disclosure).

7. VERBAL APPROACHES TO HANDLE A CHILD'S
CONCERNING NONDISCLOSURE

When a child is nondisclosing, the interviewer should first consider the possibility that this child was not abused. If the social history, the medical exam, or the child's demeanor provoke concern regarding recantation or barriers to disclosure, and the child has not responded to open questions and focused questions, the interviewer should consider whether this child can be protected in the absence of a disclosure (as with a supportive parent, and an abnormal exam). Again, a multiple session format may also be beneficial to some children in these circumstances.

If there is concern the child cannot be protected, the interviewer should make a judgment regarding the likely source of the problem and whether the child can withstand direct questions regarding barriers to disclosure. This sort of judgment is best rendered in consultation with other multidisciplinary team members. The interviewer and multidisciplinary team will need to carefully weigh possible costs in terms of compromises to the validity of the resultant information and possible mental health ramifications to the child (feeling coerced, undermining efforts to build rapport and trust with this interviewer). It is important to note that direct approaches may invalidate the interview in some legal contexts and may make it more difficult to protect this child and other children in the long run. Despite these cautions, the multidisciplinary team/ interviewer may decide to proceed with direct questioning when protection issues are at stake and/or the child is deemed to be at high risk.

Some examples of acceptable approaches, ordered in terms of increasing risk, include the following:

> When there's a concern from the start (e.g., the child has already recanted), you might try: "I'll be asking a lot of questions today. If you can't tell me the truth about one of my questions, it's OK to say so, and I won't make you answer. You can just say, 'I can't talk about that one.'"

Early in the interview, when the child is obviously embarrassed or having trouble developing rapport, the interviewer may want to comment on the discomfort and offer the child choices, for example, "I can see that it is hard for you to talk to me today. Is there something I can do to make it easier?" Try to accommodate any requests the child makes; for example, if the video is worrisome, children can hide under the counter or turn their backs to the camera; if a particular observer is worrisome, that person can leave the viewing room. If the child can't tell you how to make it easier, you can try, "It's important that you try to answer my questions, so I want to tell you about some choices. You can tell me with words, you can show me with dolls, you can write your answers on this piece of paper, or you can whisper in my ear. Does one of those choices sound OK?" If these approaches don't work, consider extending rapport development, perhaps moving to a multiple session format.

"Did someone else talk to you about what to tell me today? What did they say?"; "Is there something you're not supposed to tell me today?"

"Did anyone say something that scared you?"; "Is there someone you're afraid of?"; "What could a kid do if someone is hurting them?" You can also explore likes, dislikes, and worries with a list of people, including presumably neutral individuals along with suspected perpetrator(s).

"Did you ever tell anyone else that you had been touched? Who did you tell? What did you tell them? Is what you told that person true?" If the answer is no, "What made you change your mind about that?" or "What made you decide it wasn't true?"

"Is there something you're worried about if you tell the truth today?"; "Are you worried about something happening with (mother, alleged perpetrator) if you tell the truth today?"; "What do you think will happen if you tell the truth today?"

"What did your mother do when you told ___ about the touching?" "What did (alleged perpetrator) do when he found out you had told somebody?"

When there is a physical injury present, the interviewer may want to ask direct questions that may permit the child to rule out accidental causes. For example, "Who helps you go potty? Did it hurt when they helped?"; "Did you ever fall and hurt your pee pee?"; "Did anything get stuck in your bottom?"; or "Did you ever get medicine (or go to the doctor) for your bottom?"

When there is a concern regarding a misunderstanding or initial false accusation, the interviewer can ask children if they ever told someone they were touched in a way they didn't like. If the child responds affirmatively, the interviewer might say, "I need to know if what you told that person was true. If it's not true, that's OK, and now is a really good time to clear up any misunderstandings. If it is true, it would be helpful for me to know so I can help keep you safe. You won't get in any trouble no matter what you say. Was what you told ___ true?" If no, "So ___ didn't touch you? Thank you for clearing that up. What would you do if someone did touch you? (prevention work)."

Use the following with caution:

"I'm really worried that someone might have touched or hurt you. You don't have to tell me today, but it's important that you tell someone if something like that happened. Is there someone you could tell about things like that?"

"The doctor told me that during the exam, it looked like someone had hurt you. It's important that I know if someone hurt you, so that I can keep you safe. Did somebody hurt you?"

8. ANATOMICAL DOLLS AND NONDISCLOSURE

Some experts (Boat and Everson, 1993; Morgan, 1995) suggest that the interviewer allow the nondisclosing child to play freely with anatomical dolls. The child's behavior would be carefully observed, and the interviewer would encourage the child to provide a verbal narrative regarding his or her activities with the dolls (e.g., "What's happening there?"). It is important that the interviewer show interest in the child's activities and encourage child commentary, irrespective of whether the child is demonstrating sexual or nonsexual activity. However, the interviewer's comments should not be so frequent as to interfere with the child's ability to use the dolls.

If the child does show sexual positioning, the interviewer should ask neutral follow-up questions (e.g., "What are the dolls doing now?") to clarify the activity. Because non-abused children will occasionally exhibit sex-

By itself, sexual positioning using anatomical dolls is not diagnostic of sexual abuse.

ual positioning with anatomical dolls (see Boat & Everson, 1993, for a review), it is important to ask children where they learned about these things, before assuming something has happened to them. **Sexual positioning alone is not diagnostic of sexual abuse.** The interviewer's attempts to encourage children to verbalize what is happening and where they learned about these activities are therefore critical to making a determination regarding the likelihood of abuse. If this approach is utilized, the interviewer should be well aware that it is likely to be challenged in court, due to concerns regarding doll suggestibility. See Chapter 12, "The Use of Anatomical Dolls and Other Tools," for more detail on using dolls in child interviews.

9. CHILDREN WHO RECANT

When a child recants allegations of abuse, it is important that the child be evaluated regarding the source of the recantation. It is critical that an attempt be made to establish whether the child is recanting a false report versus a true report. Children who recant a false report may be in need of mental health services addressing the motivation for the false report. Children who recant a true report are likely in need of both mental health and child protective services. Many of the questioning approaches detailed in this chapter and the chapter on false reports will be helpful in this regard. Centers should work with their local multidisciplinary teams to establish a policy regarding assessment of children who recant. Some communities may feel more comfortable with child therapists addressing this issue, whereas others may want a child interviewer to speak with the child.

18

Interviewing the
Special Needs Child

❑ **Guideline**

When a child with special needs must be evaluated for possible
sexual abuse, the interviewer should prepare in advance to minimize the accommodations the child must make in the interview
setting. The interviewer should acquire information from people
familiar with the child to answer the following questions:

1. What is the special need?
2. How does the special need affect the child in normal situations
   (school)?
3. How will the special need affect the child's participation in the interview?

❏ **Supporting Information**

1. RANGE OF SPECIAL NEEDS

Children who may have special needs in the interviewing context include those who are not fluent in English and those with attentional problems, hyperactive behavior, emotional disturbances, learning disabilities, and developmental delays (low general intelligence or delayed acquisition of specific skills). There is very little research on how these children perform in the interviewing context. The diverse nature of this population presents a challenge to researchers and interviewers in defining the difficulties experienced by the child, as well as in defining desired accommodations to be made by the interviewer.

Because the interview is primarily a conversation, physical impairments impose only minimal constraints on the interview. With physical impairment, the use of tools may be restricted and/or the interviewer may have to assist the child to utilize tools.

The most significant special needs involve children with cognitive impairments and communication difficulties, as well as children who speak a different language. This chapter will briefly describe suggestions for interviewing children whose language or communication skills present a challenge to forensic interviewers. Children who are not fluent in English and children who have developmental disabilities will be discussed. Children who present with attention deficit disorders or hyperactive behaviors will also be mentioned briefly.

2. PREVALENCE OF SPECIAL NEEDS

In this chapter, the term *disability* will refer to children whose physical movement, speech, language comprehension, or learning is impaired. In school settings, approximately 10% of children receive special services for disabilities ("Special Education for Students With Disabilities," 1996). Half of these children have specific learning disabilities, and 25% have speech and language disorders. Two thirds of these children have more than one disability, irrespective of diagnostic labels. Most disabilities are very mild and would not interfere with the child's ability to remember or report events. Approximately 3% to 5% of children have what is known as a developmental disability, formerly referred to as mental retardation (Tharinger, Burrows-Horton, & Millea, 1990). Of this subset of disabled persons, 85% are classified as mildly impaired (IQs in the 55 to 70 range), 10% are moderately impaired, and 5% are severely or profoundly impaired (IQs below 40). The rate of abuse for disabled children may be higher than that for non-disabled children (Ammerman, van Haslett, Herson, McGonigle, & Lubetsky, 1989; Sobsey, 1994; Valenti-Hein & Schwartz, 1995; Verdugo, Bermeho, & Fuertes, 1995). Consequently, these children may make up a significant portion of the population of children presenting for child abuse interviews.

Nationally, the number of children who require special educational instruction because they are not fluent in English is on the rise. However, the prevalence of children speaking particular languages varies widely according to geographical area.

Approximately 3% to 5% of school-age children are diagnosed with attention deficit or hyperactivity disorders (American Psychiatric Association, 1994). Within this group, there exists tremendous variability in the ability to manage the disorder through medication and behavioral interventions.

3. THE IMPORTANCE OF MAKING ADAPTATIONS

Emotional or stressful situations may exacerbate a child's disability or language comprehension difficulties. With some children, exacerbation of the difficulty could prevent completion of the interview. This phenomenon is particularly common among children and adults who have cerebral palsy that interferes with their speech. The interviewer should make every effort to accommodate the environment to the child, to minimize the child's stress. The interviewer should help the child feel emotionally and physically comfortable. If the child appears anxious, the interviewer should back away from questioning and help the child to resolve the anxiety.

4. DETERMINING THE LEVEL OF ADAPTATION REQUIRED

Many special needs children can be evaluated with no modifications to the guidelines published in this document. For example, some children are bilingual and possess adequate skills in English to complete the interview without an interpreter. Some older school-age or teenage children with cognitive impairments possess the skill levels of a child 7 or older and thus can access most of the requisite cognitive skills. The more a child differs from average agemates, the more adaptations may be required. Adaptations become critically important when the special need involves cognitive or communication difficulties.

The more a child differs from average agemates, the more adaptations may be required.

For a significantly developmentally delayed child, the general model of interviewing may be appropriate, using strategies typically employed for younger or less knowledgeable children.

5. ASSESS NEEDED ADAPTATIONS AND ONLY MAKE THOSE THAT APPEAR NECESSARY

Each child is unique. The interviewer may be told that the child functions at a particular age level. However, there may be great unevenness in impairment across one person's development. For example, a child may exhibit good self-care, social skills, and vocabulary but lack the reasoning and abstracting abilities of agemates. Although language must be simplified, the interviewer should realize that children are frequently more sophisticated in what they understand than in what they can say back to us. The interviewer should treat children in an age-appropriate manner and not be condescending.

6. CONTACT INVOLVED PROFESSIONALS PRIOR TO THE EVALUATION

To appropriately adapt the interviewing environment, the interviewer should acquire information regarding the child's needs and the specific effects of any disability on the child (Baldarian, 1992). For example, the interviewer will want to know how the child communicates (pictures, words, sign language, bilingual). The interviewer will need specific information about the child's English language skills, particularly when English is a second language. School personnel are particularly helpful in this regard, as are parents. The interviewer must keep in mind that the interviewing context requires a high proficiency level, in understanding vocabulary, nuances of speech, and, ideally, production of a detailed narrative. Any adaptations required in school and home environments are likely to be required in the interviewing context as well. Unless the child is completely fluent in English, the interviewer may want an interpreter available, particularly in case the child's language skills are less available when the child is under stress.

It is also important to note that school and family sources may be biased. Parents may be struggling to accept the extent of a child's limitations. Written reports may be outdated because a child has not been tested for several years. Children who speak another language may have undiagnosed disabilities, because the language barrier interferes with identification, and/or many tests have not been standardized for use with non–English speaking populations. The interviewer should prepare for the possibility that the child may be functioning at a higher or lower level than described by others.

7. DIFFERENCES IN GATHERING BACKGROUND INFORMATION

Extra time will likely be necessary for history gathering with special needs children. These families often feel particularly vulnerable. With children from other cultures (deaf children, non–English speaking children), the family may require extra reassurance regarding the evaluation and its potential impact on the child and family. Their trust in "the system" may be lower, or their culture may prescribe a competing response to the crisis. In families of disabled children, the possible victimization may reactivate grief issues regarding children's inability to protect themselves. The grieving parent may present as demanding or angry rather than sad.

With disabled children, the interviewer should gather a history of the child's condition. Important questions include how the child is impacted and when the parents first became aware of the problem.

It is especially relevant to ask what conversations regarding the allegation might have occurred in the child's presence. This question should be asked in addition to questions about conversations with the child regarding the allegations. It is common for parents and professionals to talk about allegations in the child's presence, because they may not realize the child understands what is being said.

8. DIFFERENCES IN THE CHILD INTERVIEW

For children with very limited cognitive and language functioning, **the physical examination may be the best arena** for an interview, because children can show on their own bodies what occurred and to exactly what area of the body.

The Beginning Phase of the Interview May Need to Be Lengthened

It may be particularly important to elicit running narratives and to conduct a practice interview regarding nontraumatic events. These activities provide the interviewer with a relevant sample of the child's cognitive skills, language usage, and eagerness to please adults. The interviewer and/or interpreter can match language to the child's language. The child's descriptions can be compared to those obtained from adult caretakers. When an interpreter is being used, this section allows the interpreter to acclimate to the child's speaking or signing style. It is also critical to review and practice using ground rules, reassuring children that it is OK not to know all the answers and OK to ask the interviewer questions if they don't understand what is being said.

During Abuse-Focused Questioning, the Interviewer Should Move Slowly

The interviewer should be prepared to tolerate silence with children who have cognitive or language difficulties. These children may need more time to process a question and retrieve responses. A similar time lag occurs when an interpreter is being used. Language should be kept simple. As with younger children, complex multiple-choice questions, how or why questions, and yes/no questions can be problematic when a child has cognitive limitations. The interviewer should be watching for response biases (always answering yes, always choosing the last alternative), which could invalidate the child's responses.

In interviewing children with cognitive or communication difficulties, props such as anatomical dolls or drawings can be extremely valuable.

In interviewing children with cognitive or communication difficulties, props such as anatomical dolls or drawings can be extremely valuable adjuncts, so long as the child is capable of abstract representation. A child who is functioning below the level of the average 4-year-old probably will not be able to use a doll or drawing as a self-representation. Whenever possible, tools should be employed using the same guidelines as for the general population, for example, tools should be used only as adjuncts to verbal statements and should be used only when it is clear that the child cannot communicate effectively without assistance. For clients with limited speech, pictures or photographs may be employed as tools. Some children may be able to draw a picture to help clarify what happened. For example, one child in our experience drew a bed, with one person lying on top of another, and their arms and legs intertwined. One of the people was labeled "Dad" and the other was labeled with the child's name. The child was only able to respond to very simple verbal questions and, even then, provided minimal responses. The drawing, however, was spontaneous and arguably the result of a much less leading process for that child. With nonverbal children, pictures of the living environment and caretakers may be presented. The children can be asked if these people touched or hurt them and where they were when they got touched or hurt. As is the case with nonimpaired children, communication with tools cannot effectively substitute for statements, because the interviewer cannot be confident that the nonverbal behavior is a representation of actual past events. Tool use can provide valuable mechanisms for clarifying when the child's ability to verbally report is extremely limited. Although these approaches may not withstand courtroom scrutiny, they may provide enough information to protect the child and/or to determine that abuse is unlikely.

When children have cognitive impairments, time and date information may be difficult to acquire. As with younger children, asking the location of the event, the child's age, what the weather was like, and the time of year can provide helpful information regarding event timing.

When an interpreter is used, the primary struggle during the questioning phase is for the interviewer to maintain rapport with the child and to question quickly enough so that the child is not overly fatigued. Time lags for interpreting lengthen the interview, leading to fatigue for the child, interviewer, and interpreter. The child also may be trying to learn the non-native language and may be exerting considerable effort to understand the initial question and to check understanding with the interpreter. The interviewer may want to plan frequent breaks and should consult with the interpreter regarding any policies they may need to honor concerning frequency and length of breaks. Some companies specify that the interpreter must take a 5- to 10-minute break once every hour.

The interviewer may need to attend to cultural issues in posing the questions. For example, with deaf clients the sign for secret, private part and privacy are the same. In Spanish, some nations use different words to refer to the private parts of animals versus people. Children from several different cultures that prescribe a demure, modest female role or that proscribe against frank discussions of sex may be more comfortable showing with dolls or writing responses rather than using the words to tell what happened to them. Interpreters can be quite valuable in helping the interviewer pose questions that are culturally sensitive.

9. DOCUMENTATION

It is especially critical that evaluations of special needs children be documented in the most sophisticated manner possible. Because these children may perform less well under stress, it is less likely that they would do well in a courtroom situation. For this reason, videotaping may be critical to preserve the child's disclosure statements and demeanor.

10. WORKING WITH THE CHILD'S CARETAKERS

Treatment resources are extremely inadequate for disabled children who have been abused, and particularly for those who are engaging in sexually reactive behaviors. At the time of the debriefing, during the social history gathering, or during other portions of the evaluation, the parents may express frustration with the interviewer's performance or with other professionals assigned to help their child. The interviewer should acknowledge the caretaker's frustration and ask for feedback to improve the interviewer's interactions with the child, when appropriate. The caretakers may take a fierce advocacy stance toward professionals involved with the child. This stance may be an adaptive approach that has been developed to help the child negotiate a hostile and inadequate educational and treatment environment. The interviewer should be prepared to support the caregivers in their advocacy, while directing them to appropriate channels.

11. SOME NOTES ON WORKING WITH ADHD CHILDREN

When an interviewer is advised that a child has been diagnosed with attention deficit hyperactivity disorder (ADHD) or a related disorder, advance preparation and accommodation are necessary. The interviewer should encourage the parent to maintain the normal medication regimen on the day of the interview. The interviewer should inquire as to the best time of day for the child and schedule the interview accordingly.

As with other special needs, the interviewer should ask the parents for a history of the child's problems. Descriptions of the child's behaviors both on and off medication should be gathered. The medication and dosage level should be documented.

Interviewing these children may require a quick moving process to maintain the child's attention. Props such as dolls and drawings are sometimes helpful in this regard, although care must be taken not to overstimulate the child. For example, only one or two dolls may be used, rather than the entire set. The interviewer may want to minimize stimulation before the child enters the room, by placing many toys and stuffed animals in cabinets or out of the room. During the interview, the interviewer should work to maintain eye contact and keep the child's attention focused on the task. The evaluation may need to occur in multiple short sessions that could be scheduled on a single day or on multiple days. For example, the interviewer could talk to the child for 10 to 20 minutes, take a break to move around outside of the room, and resume with a second 10- to 20-minute session. It should be noted that some of these children perform much better in a one-on-one situation than they would in the school classroom, and they may not require changes in interviewing format.

12. SOME NOTES ON USING A LANGUAGE INTERPRETER

Language interpreters are imperative in evaluations involving deaf children and children whose native language is not English, unless the interviewer is fluent in the child's native language. Then the child may be given a choice as to which language is preferred. Language interpreters might still be necessary when conducting the interview entirely in the child's natve language, because of the need for translation to make the interview comprehensible to individuals or agencies who need the information. Interpreters may also be used when children have severe cerebral palsy that impedes their speech or brain injuries that affect speech, and with autistic or nonverbal children. The most important criterion for a competent interpreter is the ability to remain neutral. The interpreter should preferably not be a person the child has disclosed to previously or a person with a vested interest in the outcome of the evaluation.

Know the Child's Needs

With deaf children, their specific form of communication must be understood. It is important to know if they use American Sign Language, idiosyncratic signing, or signed English. The interviewer should NEVER assume that a deaf child can write in English. These children's signing skills are often far better than their written skills.

At times, the child's teacher may be willing to prepare a short video of the child in the classroom. Such videos are most useful if speech is spontaneous and child-generated, so the interviewer and interpreter can assess the child's communication style and skill level.

With children from other cultures, their ability to speak English is important to know, to make the determination regarding whether and to what extent the use of an interpreter would be appropriate. As noted earlier, the interviewer will probably want to use a language interpreter, unless the child is fully fluent in English.

When a child displays idiosyncratic speech, it is helpful to identify a neutral person familiar with the child's speech to act as an interpreter. As with other special needs children, teachers and parents are valuable resources for describing the child's needs.

Know the Interpreter

All interpreters must be comfortable speaking with children in the age ranges they work with, and must be able to tolerate sexually explicit material. The interpreter should balance a primary emphasis on verbatim interpretation with the ability to notify the interviewer when the child is not comprehending a question, or when the interviewer may want to rephrase a question due to cultural issues. With deaf interpreters, gestures and explanations may be necessary as many signs mean the same thing. The interpreter should be legally certified.

The evaluating team should develop good rapport with the interpreter.

It is helpful for the evaluating team to develop a good rapport with the interpreter. Using a few interpreters on a rotating basis can increase everyone's comfort and improve the child's evaluation. It is very helpful to provide the interpreter with an understanding of usual procedures during the evaluation and the evaluator's expectations for the interpreter's role. The interviewer may want to discuss the dynamics of sexual abuse in general, and of this case in particular, to facilitate the interpreter's preparedness. It may be necessary to repeatedly emphasize that the interpreter should not discuss the allegation with the child while the interviewer is out of the room or add his or her opinions in talking with the child. Many programs write down these expectations and have interpreters sign an agreement indicating their intent to comply with these stipulations. If an interpreter's personal issues appear to be interfering with the evaluation, it is appropriate to reschedule or to request another interpreter to come on an emergent basis. Rotating a few interpreters prevents these sorts of problems from arising in many cases, because expectations are clear based on prior experience.

Improving the Triangular Relationship

When using an interpreter, there is more than one adult in the room, and more than one adult the child must trust in order to feel safe relating details of abuse. It is helpful for the interpreter to have time with the child prior to the evaluation. This can happen while social and/or medical history are being gathered from the child's caretakers. Information gained from the parent or guardian regarding the child's communication style should also be related to the interpreter.

Deciding where everyone should sit can take time. If the interview is being videotaped, it is important to make sure all parties are visible on the tape. If signing is being used, both the hands of the child and the hands of the interpreter should be on the video. All parties should be seated at comfortable distances so all are at ease. All parties should be identified by name on tape and/or in the written report.

Questions should be asked directly to the child, and the interviewer should maintain eye contact with the child. There is no need to say to the interpreter, "Would you ask her . . ." before each question. The interviewer's use of body language may make it difficult for the interpreter, but may be seen as quite positive by the child, particularly deaf children.

13. AUGMENTIVE COMMUNICATION

Augmentation refers to the use of a communication tool or aid, typically a computer keyboard or A-to-Z spelling board. On a broad level, glasses and hearing aids are augmentive devices. Some children can answer questions with a great deal of sophistication using a keyboard to type out the answer. Statements from these children should not be treated any differently from statements made by non-impaired children.

Some children communicate with picture boards that allow a very limited range of responses. Interviewing with these aids may require an interpreter who fully understands the aid and the child's ability to use the aid.

As with any special needs child, the interviewer must ascertain the child's specific difficulty and why a keyboard addresses that difficulty. The interviewer should also know in advance what type of keyboard is used, and how capable the child is of independent language production. When necessary, interpreters familiar with the child, but who are not involved with the allegation (e.g., not the person to whom the child initially disclosed), should attend the evaluation.

14. FACILITATED COMMUNICATION

Facilitated communication refers to situations in which a child requires direct assistance by another person to use a keyboard or spelling board. The child's facilitator purportedly assists by stabilizing motor movements. There is a wide range of involvement by the facilitator, from subtle contact at the child's elbow, to firmly gripping the child's hand in such a way that it is not clear who is making the keyboard letter selection. Facilitated communication is quite controversial (*Child Abuse & Neglect*, Special Issue on Facilitated Communication, 1994). Before evaluating a child who uses facilitated communication, the interviewer will want to know:

- Can anyone facilitate for the child?
- Could the interviewer facilitate, with preliminary training? If so, the communication is functionally augmentive.
- Is there a facilitator available who is not involved in the allegation?

The interviewer may also design simple tests of the child's ability to communicate independently, such as exposing the child to a picture of an object, without the facilitator in the room, then have the facilitator return and ask the child to type the name of the object.

Because this technique is so controversial, emotions can run high during the assessment process. The interviewer should remain neutral and open to all possible interpretations regarding the source of the child's statements. It is important to note that courts have been inconsistent in accepting statements made via facilitated communication.

Coping With Custody and Visitation Disputes

❏ **Guideline**

Evaluating allegations of child sexual abuse in the context of custody and visitation disputes can be especially challenging and time-consuming. The interviewer should allow extra time for these evaluations and should be cautious in making contact and visitation recommendations.

❏ **Supporting Information**

1. MANY DIVORCES DO NOT INVOLVE CUSTODY
   AND VISITATION DISPUTES

Most often, when an allegation of sexual abuse surfaces in a divorced family, the child's evaluation should be no different than that for any alleged victim. Special procedures are necessary only when it is clear that a family is embroiled in a custody or visitation dispute, or when a divorced parent seems overly invested in negative feelings toward the former spouse.

2. THE PREVALENCE OF FALSE ALLEGATIONS IS LOW, EVEN WITH DISPUTING PARENTS

The most thorough study to date regarding allegations of sexual abuse in cases of custody and visitation disputes included 9,000 families served by eight domestic relations courts (Thoennes & Tjaden, 1990). In this study, less than 2% of divorce and custody cases involved false allegations of sexual abuse. Of these, about 14% were felt to be deliberate false allegations. It is noteworthy that Thoennes and Tjaden found that substantiation rates for allegations involving custody disputes (slightly less than 50%) were comparable to substantiation rates of other sexual abuse cases (53%; Jones & McGraw, 1987). Some studies have cited higher rates of false allegation in custody and visitation disputes, but those studies involved small samples (e.g., less than 20 families) and criteria for designating cases "false" versus "valid" were unclear (Blush & Ross, 1987; Faller, Corwin, & Olafson, 1993; Green, 1991; Jones & McGraw, 1987; Jones & Selg, 1988; Kaplan & Kaplan, 1981).

3. WHY DO ALLEGATIONS OF SEXUAL ABUSE OCCUR IN CUSTODY AND VISITATION DISPUTES?

Thoennes and Tjaden (1990) indicated that allegations of abuse were six times more likely during a custody or visitation dispute than at other times during the family life cycle. Parental separation provokes strong emotions, leaves both parents with heightened awareness of unmet needs, and may reduce the parents' ability to supervise the child. The same factors that produce heightened risk of child sexual abuse make it more likely that parents will divorce. Domestic violence, parental drug and alcohol

Anger at the former spouse can provide motivation to falsify or misinterpret actions.

abuse, and parental psychopathology are associated with both risk of divorce and child sexual abuse. On the other hand, anger at the former spouse provides motivation to falsify or misinterpret actions.

Faller (1991) provides four explanations for abuse allegations surfacing in the context of a custody and visitation dispute:

a. **The nonoffending parent discovers the abuse and divorces** the offending parent. Obviously, in these cases the nonoffending parent will not want the child who had experienced abuse residing in the home of the offender and may instigate a custody/visitation dispute to protect the child.

b. There is **long-standing abuse,** which is revealed when the perpetrator has less opportunity to enforce secrecy following a divorce or when a child no longer fears family dissolution because of disclosure (because the family has already dissolved). The child may also disclose out of fear of being alone with the offender during visitation.

c. **Sexual abuse is precipitated by marital dissolution.** The offending parent may be seeking a vicarious connection to the ex-spouse or may be seeking vicarious revenge.

d. There may be a **false allegation,** precipitated by a vengeful parent, a vengeful child, or a misunderstanding based on biases against the accused offender.

4. DIFFERENCES IN GATHERING BACKGROUND INFORMATION

In addition to the normal history gathering process, the interviewer is likely to be provided with extra reports and lengthy interviews with law enforcement and the nonoffending parent. The additional information is a primary reason these evaluations are so time-consuming. The interviewer should review all reports, focusing on the child's previous disclosures and the circumstances that elicited the disclosure. The interviewer should also seek information regarding prior evaluations for abuse.

The nonoffending parent and other persons seeking custody of the child should be asked how they determined that this child had been victimized. These caretakers should be asked to relate their conversations with the child about alleged abuse and should also be asked their response to the allegations. The interviewer will want to carefully assess whether the parent's focus is on the child's well-being, or on the parent's feelings toward the former spouse. The interviewer will want to assess whether the parent has reached a logical conclusion, given the available information, or whether there are alternative explanations for the child's actions and statements.

All of the foregoing information should be carefully documented in the interviewer's report.

5. INTERVIEWING THE ACCUSED PERPETRATOR

Contacting the accused perpetrator can endanger a child and might interfere with the investigation.

Generally, it is not recommended that interviewers contact the accused perpetrator unless they have the explicit permission of law enforcement. Contacting the accused perpetrator can endanger the child and might interfere with the investigation. Typically, law enforcement officers will assume that it is their role to contact and interview the alleged perpetrator. At times, law enforcement will have already interviewed the suspect and can provide information regarding the accused's perspective when the interviewer is not permitted contact with the accused.

If law enforcement approves contact between the interviewer and the accused, the interviewer should contact the accused to include that person's perspective on the family history and on the current allegations, given the potential for bias in a parental dispute. Faller (1997) notes that the accused person may be able to provide an explanation to account for the child's statements and that a conversation with the accused provides a safeguard for the interviewer against absorbing the biases of the accusing parent.

6. DIFFERENCES IN THE CHILD INTERVIEW

Faller (1990b) recommends that the child be brought to the interview by a neutral party. It is the experience of members of this committee that when a child is living with a biased parent, having a neutral party accompany the child may not eliminate bias and may eliminate an important source of information regarding parental bias. Often the parent's biases become clear only as the custodial parent is interviewed and becomes comfortable with the interviewer. Finally, it is often not possible to know in advance who is neutral and who is not, because divorces sometimes polarize entire families, and professional communities as well. Thus, it is acceptable for the child to be brought by the nonoffending parent unless there is evidence in advance that this person is coaching the child.

During the initial phases of the interview, the interviewer should **ask questions about all households the child regularly visits.** Activities, routines, and perceptions of caretakers are fruitful avenues of exploration. Relationships with both parents before and after the abuse accusation should be explored.

During the middle phase of the interview, the alleged victim's **ability to provide experiential detail is even more important than usual.** The interviewer should focus on whether the **child's language** in describing abuse is consistent with language development skills displayed during other portions of the interview. In addition, the possiblity of **coaching, pressuring, or bias** on the part of each set of caretakers should be directly explored through questioning the child. See Chapters 16 and 17, "Errors in Children's Reports," and "The Nondisclosing Child," for more detail.

7. THE EVALUATION MAY NEED TO OCCUR
OVER MULTIPLE SESSIONS

Because the background information is more complex and the interview includes additional components, a thorough evaluation may require more than one session. In these cases, the interviewer could consider gathering background information in one session and interviewing in the second session, or breaking up the interview, focusing on routines in various households and caretaker relationships in one interview, with abuse-focused questioning, questions regarding coaching, and closure in the second interview. See Chapter 5, "Single Versus Multiple Interviewers," for more details.

8. MULTIDISCIPLINARY TEAM EVALUATION IS MORE IMPORTANT IN THESE CASES

Because the interviewer may be restricted from contacting the accused perpetrator, an important perspective may not be included in the sexual abuse evaluation. The interviewer will rely on law enforcement, and possibly psychologists, to include the accused parent's perspective in the overall determination regarding visitation and treatment (Myers, 1989–1990).

When the nonoffending parent's presentation is concerning or when the sexual abuse evaluation is inconclusive, the interviewer may need to request a custody study. These studies frequently include psychological evaluation of both parents, and parent–child interactions as well. Typically, there will be specialists in the community who are experienced in conducting thorough custody evaluations. At other times, the interviewer may need to refer the family to a therapist who is skilled in managing unsubstantiated allegations of sexual abuse (Hewitt, 1991). The interviewer or the center where the interviewer works should develop relationships with these professionals to facilitate referrals and consultation on difficult cases.

Ultimately, final decisions regarding custody and visitation will be made by either child protection workers or the court, and the sexual abuse evaluation may be only one of many sets of data considered by these entities.

9. THE INTERVIEWER SHOULD BE CIRCUMSPECT IN MAKING RECOMMENDATIONS

In a typical sexual abuse evaluation, the interviewer, and possibly the examiner, as community experts on child sexual abuse, will be asked to provide recommendations regarding treatment for the child and contact with the alleged perpetrator. In sexual abuse evaluations that also involve disputed custody or visitation, there may be missing data. Consequently, the interviewer should be cautious in making recommendations for these cases (Corwin, Berliner, Goodman, Goodwin, & White, 1987).

> *The interviewer should make it clear that all recommendations are made only on the basis of available information.*

It is suggested that the interviewer make it clear that **all recommendations are made only on the basis of available information** and that the recommendations may be on an interim basis, pending further evaluation and investigation. These caveats are particularly important when there are concerns regarding the quality of the child's disclosure, coaching, or bias on the part of nonoffending caretakers who are also seeking custody. Caveats are less necessary when these concerns are not present.

All recommendations regarding contact should be flagged as preliminary, pending further investigation or evaluation.

The interviewer may want to recommend a custody study to further assess the allegation and to assess the child's ability to tolerate visitation with the alleged perpetrator. The custody study could include psychological evaluations of the child and all disputing adults, adult–child interactions, offender evaluations, and polygraphs of all disputing parties regarding attempts to influence the child's statements. It is noted that the custody evaluator may want to meet with the child to make a preliminary assessment of the child's ability to tolerate adult–child interactions with the alleged offender. The child may experience such contact as a betrayal of trust, once sexual abuse has been disclosed. The interviewer and custody evaluator may need to consult regarding this issue.

Treatment recommendations should include a focus on the impact of the divorce and the ensuing dispute on the child. In cases of possible false disclosure or parental bias/coaching, treatment should focus first on the divorce and secondarily on possible sexual abuse. In cases in which allegations are unsubstantiated, the treatment provider should be skilled in assessing and managing the family dynamics, as well as in helping the child (Hewitt, 1991).

APPENDIX A

Core Literature for Child Interviewers

❑ Books

Doris, J. (Ed.). (1991). *The suggestibility of children's recollections: Implications for eyewitness testimony.* Washington, DC: American Psychological Association.

Faller, K. (1996). *Evaluating children suspected of having been sexually abused: The APSAC Study Guides, 2.* Thousand Oaks, CA: Sage.

Fontes, L. A. (Ed.). (1995). *Sexual abuse in nine North American cultures: Treatment and prevention.* Thousand Oaks, CA: Sage.

Goodman, G. S., & Bottoms, B. L. (Eds.). (1993). *Child victims, child witnesses: Understanding and improving testimony.* New York: Guilford Press.

Melton, G. B., Petrila, J., Poythress, N. G., & Slobogin, C. (1987). *Psychological evaluations for the courts: A handbook for mental health professionals and lawyers.* New York: Guilford Press.

Morgan, M. (1995). *How to interview sexual abuse victims.* Thousand Oaks, CA: Sage.

Stern, P. (1997). *Preparing and presenting expert testimony in child abuse litigation: A guide for expert witnesses and attorneys.* Thousand Oaks, CA: Sage.

Walker, A. G. (1994). *Handbook on questioning children: A linguistic perspective.* Washington, DC: American Bar Association Center on Children and the Law.

❑ Articles

American Professional Society on the Abuse of Children (APSAC). (1990). *Guidelines for psychosocial evaluation of suspected sexual abuse in young children.* Chicago: APSAC.

American Professional Society on the Abuse of Children (APSAC). (1995). *Practice guidelines: Use of anatomical dolls in child sexual abuse assessments.* Chicago: APSAC.

Baladerian, N. (1992). *Interviewing skills to use with abuse victims who have developmental disability.* Culver City, CA: Abuse and Personal Rights Program.

Brazelton, T. B. (1992). *Touchpoints, the essential reference: Your child's emotional and behavioral development.* Reading, MA: Addison-Wesley.

Bruck, M., Ceci, S. J., Francoeur, E., & Renick, A. (1995). Anatomically detailed dolls do not facilitate preschoolers' reports of a pediatric examination involving genital touching. *Journal of Experimental Psychology: Applied, 1*(2), 95–109.

Bussey, K. (1992). Lying and truthfulness: Children's definitions, standards and evaluative reactions. *Child Development, 63,* 129–137.

Ceci, S. J., & Bruck, M. (1993). Suggestibility of the child witness: A historical review and synthesis. *Psychological Bulletin, 113*(3), 403–439.

Corwin, D. L., Berliner, L., Goodman, G., Goodwin, J., & White, S. (1987). Child sexual abuse and custody disputes: No easy answers. *American Journal of Psychotherapy, 45*(1), 113–123.

Everson, M., & Boat, B. (1994). Putting the anatomical doll controversy in perspective: An examination of the major uses and criticisms of the dolls in sexual abuse evaluations. *Child Abuse & Neglect, 18,* 113–130.

Faller, K. C. (1996). Interviewing children who may have been abused: A historical perspective and overview of controversies. *Child Maltreatment, 1*(2), 83–95.

Faller, K. C., Corwin, D., & Olafson, E. (1993). Literature review: Research on false allegations of sexual abuse in divorce. *The APSAC Advisor, 6*(3).

Finkelhor, D., & Brown, A. (1985). The traumatic impacts of child sexual abuse: A conceptualization. *American Journal of Orthopsychiatry, 55,* 530–541.

Goodman, G. S., & Aman, C. (1990). Children's use of anatomically detailed dolls to recount an event. *Child Development, 61,* 1859–1871.

Gordon, B. N., Ornstein, P. A., Nida, R. E., Follmer, A., Crenshaw, M. C., & Albert, G. (1993). Does the use of dolls facilitate children's memory of visits to the doctor? *Applied Cognitive Psychology, 7,* 459–474.

Hewitt, S., & Friedrich, W. (1995). Assessment and management of abuse allegations with very young children. In T. Ney (Ed.), *True and false allegations of child sexual abuse.* New York: Brunner/Mazel.

Kendall-Tackett, K. A., Williams, L. M., & Finkelhor, D. (1993). Impact of sexual abuse on children: A review and synthesis of recent empirical studies. *Psychological Bulletin, 113,* 164–180.

Leichtman, M. D., & Ceci, S. J. (1995). The effects of stereotypes and suggestions on preschoolers' reports. *Developmental Psychology, 31*(4), 568–578.

Perry, N. W. (1992). How children remember and why they forget. *The APSAC Advisor, 5*(3), 1–2, 13–15.

Sorenson, E., Bottoms, B., & Perona, A. (1997). *Handbook on intake and forensic interviewing in the Children's Advocacy Center setting.* Washington, DC: Office of Juvenile Justice and Delinquency Prevention.

Sorenson, T., & Snow, B. (1991). How children tell: The process of disclosure in child sexual abuse. *Child Welfare, 70,* 3–15.

Steward, M. S., Bussey, K., Goodman, G. S., & Saywitz, K. J. (1993). Implications of developmental research for interviewing children. *Child Abuse & Neglect, 17,* 25–37.

Summit, R. C. (1983). The child sexual abuse accommodation syndrome. *Child Abuse & Neglect, 7*, 177–193.

Tharinger, D., Burrows-Horton, C., & Millea, S. (1990). Sexual abuse and exploitation of children and adults with mental retardation and other handicaps. *Child Abuse & Neglect, 14*, 301–312.

Thoennes, N., & Tjaden, P. G. (1990). The extent, nature, and validity of sexual abuse allegations in custody/visitation disputes. *Child Abuse & Neglect, 14*, 151–163.

van der Kolk, B. (1994). The body keeps the score: Memory and the evolving psychobiology of posttraumatic stress. *Harvard Review of Psychiatry, 1*, 253–265.

Warren, A. R., & McGough, L. S. (1996). Research on children's suggestibility: Implications for the investigative interview. *Criminal Justice and Behavior, 23*(2), 269–303.

C. A. R. E. S. Northwest Program Social History Questionnaire

Your Name _____ Your Relation to Child _____
CHILD'S NAME_____ DATE OF BIRTH _____
Name of biological father _____ Date of birth _____
Name of biological mother _____ Date of birth _____
Name of brothers/sisters _____ Date of birth _____
_____ Date of birth _____
_____ Date of birth _____
_____ Date of birth _____
_____ Date of birth _____
Name of stepfather_____ Date of birth _____
Name of stepmother _____ Date of birth _____
Name of stepbrothers/sisters_____ Date of birth _____
_____ Date of birth _____
_____ Date of birth _____
_____ Date of birth _____
_____ Date of birth _____
Has child's mother been married before? _____( ) No   ( ) Yes   # times_____
To whom? _____ Date(s) _____
Divorced?_____ Date(s) _____
Has child's father been married before? _____( ) No   ( ) Yes   # times_____
To whom? _____ Date(s) _____
Divorced?_____ Date(s) _____

Please list all addresses where your child has <u>ever</u> lived, who else lived with the child, and dates of residence at each location:

ADDRESS   WHO LIVED HERE?   DATES RESIDED

_____

_____

_____

_____

_____

_____

_____

_____

Has your child ever been in foster care?   ( ) No   ( ) Yes
When? _____

Name of foster care giver (if known)_____

_____

_____

Please list other people who have taken care of your child (babysitters, relatives, daycare providers, etc.)

NAME   RELATION   DATES

_____

_____

_____

_____

_____

_____

_____

If parents work outside of the home, what are work hours?_____

_____

Have there been any prior concerns of physical and/or sexual abuse to this child or siblings?   ( ) No   ( ) Yes

If so, please describe briefly _____

_____

Has your child seen adults hit one another?   ( ) No   ( ) Yes

If yes, please describe briefly _____

_____

Has your child seen adults nude?

( ) No   ( ) Yes

Has your child ever walked in while adults were having sex?

( ) No   ( ) Yes

If yes, please describe briefly _____

_____

What nudity or sexual activity might your child have seen on TV, in movies, on videotapes, or in magazines?_____

_____

Is there any pornography in your home?

( ) No   ( ) Yes

Is there any pornography in homes your child visits?

( ) No   ( ) Yes

Child's school_____ Grade_____ Teacher_____

( ) Doing well   ( ) Average   ( ) Doing poorly

Any learning problems?   ( ) No   ( ) Yes
Special Education placement?   ( ) No   ( ) Yes

Does your child have difficulties getting along with teachers or other adults?

( ) No   ( ) Yes

If yes, please explain_____

Does your child have difficulties getting along with other children?

( ) No   ( ) Yes

If yes, please explain_____

Has your child been or is he/she currently in counseling?

( ) No   ( ) Yes

Therapist _____
Address _____
Phone #_____

Have other family members been (or are currently) in counseling?

( ) No   ( ) Yes

Have any of these behaviors in your child been a concern?

( ) No ( ) Yes   Sleep problems
( ) No ( ) Yes   Nightmares
( ) No ( ) Yes   Fear of people, places, situations
( ) No ( ) Yes   Aggressiveness, hitting others
( ) No ( ) Yes   Sexualized behavior or play
( ) No ( ) Yes   Withdrawal
( ) No ( ) Yes   Lying
( ) No ( ) Yes   Stealing
( ) No ( ) Yes   Anger (tantrums, foul language)
( ) No ( ) Yes   Sadness (lasting more than a few hours)
( ) No ( ) Yes   Nervous habits (nail biting, picking skin)
( ) No ( ) Yes   Eating problems
( ) No ( ) Yes   Changes in mood or routines

Other concerns _____

_____

What discipline is used at home?

( ) No ( ) Yes   Spanking   With?_____
( ) No ( ) Yes   Time out
( ) No ( ) Yes   Taking away privileges
( ) No ( ) Yes   Other (please list)

_____   _____

_____   _____

_____

Who bathes your child?_____

Who helps toilet your child?_____

Who puts your child to bed?_____

With whom does your child sleep?_____

Have there been any other significant stresses in the family (such as a death, major illness, conflict between family members, job loss, move, etc.) over the last year? Please explain:

_____

_____

_____

_____

APPENDIX C

Sources for Dolls and Drawings

Hylands Anatomical Dolls, Inc.
4463 Torrance Blvd.
Torrance, CA 90503
(800) 333-4157

Child Guidance Center
2525 East 22nd Street
Cleveland, OH 44115
(216) 696-5800
Sara Hendrix

Migima Designs
P.O. Box 5217
Portland, OR 97208
(503) 244-0044

Teach-A-Bodies
P.O. Box 10144
Fort Worth, TX 76185
(800) 203-3143

Forensic Mental Health Associates
Anatomical Drawings
7513 Pointview Circle
Orlando, FL 32836-6336
(407) 351-2308

Eymann Dolls
3645 Scarsdale Court
Sacramento, CA 95827
(916) 362-8503

Sara Ann's Country Store
"Just Right Dolls"
c/o Monroe Enterprises Drawer 479
Trenton, FL 32693
 (904) 463-2231

Uniquity
215 4th Street
Galt, CA 95632
(800) 521-7771

Ther-A-Play Products
P.O. Box 2030
Lodi, CA 95241
(800) 308-6749

Kidsrights
10100 Park Cedar Drive
Charlotte, NC 28210
(800) 892-KIDS

Anatomical Dolls
Carol Pederson, Designer
20075 SW Imperial
Aloha, OR 97006
(503) 642-1203

This list is an expanded version of a list provided by the National Resource Center on Child Sexual Abuse. The list does not constitute an endorsement for particular companies. Rather, the list is provided to increase access and choice.

C. A. R. E. S. Protective Order

IN THE CIRCUIT COURT FOR THE STATE OF OREGON
FOR THE COUNTY OF_____

```
_____ )
_____ ) _____          Case No.
__ Plaintiff, _____ )
_____ )
VS. _____ )
_____ ) _____          ORDER TO PRODUCE AND
_____ ) _____          PROTECTIVE ORDER
__ Defendant. _____ )
```

Counsel for_____is requesting
production of records pertaining to a child abuse examination of
_____ conducted at CHILD ABUSE RESPONSE AND EVALUATION
SERVICE (C. A. R. E. S.) PROGRAM of Emanuel Hospital and Health Center on
_____. Because these records may be subject to
confidentiality provisions of ORS 419A.170, 419B.035, and 419B.195 concerning
reports and evaluations of possible child abuse, and the court having taken judicial
notice of the especially sensitive content of these requested records,

IT IS HEREBY ORDERED that a true and correct copy of the records be produced
by C. A. R. E. S. Program to _____(Name),
_____ (Address) SUBJECT TO THE
FOLLOWING RESTRICTIONS:

1. All records obtained under this order shall be in the constructive custody of the court. The records shall be returned to court or to the C. A. R. E. S. Program of Emanuel Hospital and Health Center at the conclusion of this proceeding or within 40 days after the judgment order is signed by the court.

2. Records obtained under this protective order may not be viewed or otherwise used except in connection with representation of a party in the above-entitled proceeding. Any other use or viewing of these records is not authorized and shall be deemed a violation of this protective order.

3. None of the records produced may be duplicated or copied by parties or counsel. No transcripts of videotapes may be transcribed or prepared. It shall be the responsibility of counsel obtaining a videotape or photograph covered by this protective order to exercise due diligence to ensure that no unauthorized use or viewing of the videotape or photographs occurs. Counsel shall not permit any person to view or possess any record covered by this protective order without notifying that person of the existence and requirements of this order.

4. Reproductions of videotapes and photographs for release to counsel will be made solely by or under the direction of the staff at Emanuel Hospital and Health Center. Copies of PAGE videotapes and/or photographs will be produced only when an express request from counsel accompanies service of this order.

5. Counsel appearing *ex parte* and presenting this order for the court's signature shall have so notified all other counsel of record in this proceeding and the Medical Records Department of Emanuel Hospital and Health Center. Prior requests, whether by subpoena or otherwise, will be insufficient notice that production of videotapes and/or photographs has been requested by counsel and approved by the court.

6. All reasonable expenses incurred in the production of these records shall be the responsibility of the party seeking production. Payment is required at the time of production.

DATED this _____ day of _____ 199____.

_____
        Circuit Court Judge

ORDER PREPARED BY:
Richard E. Talbott Oregon State Bar No. 77370
Hallmark, Keating & Abbott, P.C.
One Southwest Columbia, Suite 800
Portland, Oregon 97258
Of Attorneys for C. A. R. E. S. Program—
Emanuel Hospital and Health Center

References

APSAC. (1995). *Practice guidelines: Use of anatomical dolls in child sexual abuse assessments.* Chicago: Author.

American Psychiatric Association. (1994). *Diagnostic and statistical manual of mental disorders, 4th ed. (DSM-IV).* Washington, DC: Author.

Ammerman, R., van Haslett, V., Herson, M., McGonigle, J., & Lubetsky, M. (1989). Abuse and neglect in psychiatrically hospitalized multihandicapped children. *Child Abuse & Neglect, 13,* 335–343.

Baker-Ward, L., Gordon, B. N., Ornstein, P. A., Larus, D. M., & Clubb, P. A. (1993). Young children's long-term retention of a pediatric exam. *Child Development, 64,* 1519–1533.

Baldarian, N. (1992). *Interviewing skills to use with abuse victims who have developmental disabilities.* Culver City, CA: Abuse and Personal Rights Program.

Bandura, A. (1991). Social cognitive theory of moral thought and action. In W. M. Kurtines & J. L. Gewirtz (Eds.), *Handbook of moral behavior and development* (Vol. 1, pp. 45–103). Hillsdale, NJ: Erlbaum.

Batterman-Faunce, J. M., & Goodman, G. S. (1993). Effects of context on the accuracy and suggestibility of child witnesses. In G. S. Goodman & B. L. Bottoms (Eds.), *Child victims, child witnesses: Understanding and improving testimony.* New York: Guilford Press.

Berliner, L. (1990). Guidelines for psychosocial evaluation of suspected sexual abuse in young children. Chicago: APSAC.

Blush, G. J., & Ross, K. L. (1987). Sexual allegations in divorce: The SAID syndrome. *Conciliation Court Review, 25*(1), 1–11.

Boat, B. W. (1995). The relationship between violence to children and violence to animals: An ignored link? *Journal of Interpersonal Violence, 10*(2), 229–235.

227

Boat, B. W., & Everson, M. D. (1988). Interviewing young children with anatomical dolls. *Child Welfare, 67,* 336–352.

Boat, B. W., & Everson, M. D. (1993). The use of anatomical dolls in sexual abuse evaluations: Current research and practice. In G. S. Goodman & B. L. Bottoms (Eds.), *Child victims, child witnesses: Understanding and improving testimony.* New York: Guilford Press.

Brainerd, C., & Ornstein, P. A. (1991). Children's memory for witnessed events: The developmental backdrop. In J. Doris (Ed.), *The suggestibility of children's recollections* (pp. 92–105). Washington, DC: American Psychological Association.

Brazelton, T. B. (1992). *Touchpoints, the essential reference: Your child's emotional and behavioral development.* Reading, MA: Addison-Wesley.

Brennan, M., & Brennan, R. (1988). *Strange language: Child victims under cross examination.* Wagga Wagga, Australia: Charles Sturt University-Riverina.

Bruck, M., Ceci, S. J., Francoeur, E., & Barr, R. (1995). "I hardly cried when I got my shot!": Influencing children's reports about a visit to their pediatrician. *Child Development, 66,* 193–208.

Bruck, M., Ceci, S. J., Francoeur, E., & Renick, A. (1995). Anatomically detailed dolls do not facilitate preschoolers' reports of a pediatric examination involving genital touching. *Journal of Experimental Psychology: Applied, 1*(2), 95–109.

Bussey, K. (1992). Lying and truthfulness: Children's definitions, standards, and evaluative reactions. *Child Development, 63,* 129–137.

Bussey, K., Lee, K., & Grimbeek, E. J. (1993). Lies and secrets: Implications for children's reporting of sexual abuse. In G. S. Goodman & B. L. Bottoms (Eds.), *Child victims, child witnesses: Understanding and improving testimony.* New York: Guilford Press.

Bussey, K., Lee, K., & Ross, C. (1991, April). Factors influencing children's lying and truthfulness. In M. De Simone & M. Toglia (Chairs), *Lying and truthfulness among young children: Implications for their participation in legal proceedings.* Symposium presented at the Society for Research in Child Development, Seattle, WA.

California Attorney General's Office. (1994). *Child Victim Witness Investigative Pilot Project: Research and evaluation final report.* Sacramento, CA: Author.

Cantlon, J., Payne, G., & Erbaugh, C. (1996). Outcome-based practice: Disclosure rates of child sexual abuse comparing allegation blind and allegation informed structured interviews. *Child Abuse & Neglect, 20*(11), 1113–1120.

Ceci, S. J., & Bruck, M. (1993). Suggestibility of the child witness: A historical review and synthesis. *Psychological Bulletin, 113*(3), 403–439.

Ceci, S. J., & Bruck, M. (1995). *Jeopardy in the courtroom: A scientific analysis of children's testimony.* Washington, DC: American Psychological Association.

Ceci, S. J., Huffman, M. L. C., Smith, E., & Loftus, E. (1994). Repeatedly thinking about a non-event: Source misattributions among preschoolers. *Consciousness & Cognition, 3,* 388–407.

Ceci, S. J., Leichtman, M. D., & White, T. (1995). *Interviewing preschoolers: Remembrance of things planted.* Unpublished manuscript.

Ceci, S. J., Loftus, E. F., Leichtman, M. D., & Bruck, M. (1994). The possible role of source misattributions in the creation of false beliefs among preschoolers. *International Journal of Clinical and Experimental Hypnosis, 17*(4), 304–319.

Ceci, S. J., Ross, D. F., & Toglia, M. P. (1987a). Age differences in suggestibility: Narrowing the uncertainties. In S. Ceci, M. Toglia, & D. Ross (Eds.), *Children's Eyewitness Memory* (pp. 79–91). New York: Springer-Verlag.

Ceci, S. J., Ross, D. F., & Toglia, M. P. (1987b). Suggestibility of children's memory: Psycholegal implications. *Journal of Experimental Psychology: General, 116*, 38–49.

Clarke-Stewart, A., Thompson, W., & Lepore, S. (1989, May). Manipulating children's interpretations through interrogation. Paper presented at the biennial meeting of the Society for Research on Child Development, Kansas City, MO.

Collins, A., Brown, J. S., & Hollum, A. (1991). Cognitive apprenticeship: Making thinking visible. *American Educator* (Winter), 6–46.

Corwin, D. L., Berliner, L., Goodman, G., Goodwin, J., & White, S. (1987). Child sexual abuse and custody disputes: No easy answers. *Journal of Interpersonal Violence, 2*(1), 91–105.

DeLoache, J. (1995). The use of dolls in interviewing young children. In M. S. Zaragoza, J. R. Graham, G. C. N. Hall, R. Hirschman, & Y. S. Beh-Porath (Eds.), *Memory and testimony in the child witness.* Newbury Park, CA: Sage.

Dent, H. (1982). The effects of interviewing strategies on the results of interviews with child witnesses. In A. Trankell (Ed.), *Reconstructing the past: The role of psychologists in criminal trials* (pp. 278–297). Deventer, the Netherlands: Kluwer.

Dent, H. R. (1991). Experimental studies of interviewing child witnesses. In J. Doris (Ed.), *The suggestibility of children's recollections* (pp. 92–105). Washington, DC: American Psychological Association.

Devitt, M. K., Honts, C. R., Gillund, B. E., Amato, S. L., Peters, D. P., & Norton, M. (1994, April). *A study of the willingness of children to make false accusations about a serious matter in a realistic setting.* Paper presented at the meeting of the American Psychology and Law Society, Santa Fe, NM.

Everson, M., & Boat, B. (1989). False allegations of sexual abuse by children and adolescents. *Journal of the American Academy of Child and Adolescent Psychiatry, 28*, 230–235.

Faller, K. (1990a). Types of questions for children alleged to have been sexually abused. *The APSAC Advisor, 3*(2), 1ff.

Faller, K. C. (1990b). *Understanding child sexual maltreatment.* Newbury Park, CA: Sage.

Faller, K. C. (1991). Possible explanations for child sexual abuse allegations in divorce. *American Journal of Orthopsychiatry, 6*, 86–91.

Faller, K. C. (1996a). *Evaluating children suspected of having been sexually abused: The APSAC Study Guides (Vol. 2).* Thousand Oaks, CA: Sage.

Faller, K. C. (1996b). Interviewing children who may have been abused: A historical perspective and overview of controversies. *Child Maltreatment, 1*(2), 83–95.

Faller, K. C. (1997, January). *Assessment of abuse allegations within the context of divorce and child custody disputes.* Paper presented at the San Diego Conference on Responding to Child Maltreatment, San Diego: CA.

Faller, K. C., Corwin, D., & Olafson, E. (1993). Literature review: Research on false allegations of sexual abuse in divorce. *The APSAC Advisor, 6*(3).

Farrar, M. J., & Goodman, G. S. (1992). Developmental changes in event memory. *Child Development, 63*, 173–187.

Finkelhor, D. (Ed.). (1986). *Sourcebook on child sexual abuse.* Beverly Hills, CA: Sage.

Finkelhor, D., & Brown, A. (1985). The traumatic impact of child sexual abuse: A conceptualization. *American Journal of Orthopsychiatry, 55*, 530–541.

Fivush, R. (1993). Developmental perspectives on autobiographical recall. In G. S. Goodman & B. L. Bottoms (Eds.), *Child victims, child witnesses: Understanding and improving testimony.* New York: Guilford Press.

Fivush, R., & Hammond, N. R. (1990). Autobiographical memory across the pre-school years. In R. Fivush & J. A. Hudson (Eds.), *Knowing and remembering in young children* (pp. 223–248). New York: Cambridge University Press.

Flin, R. (1991). Commentary: A grand memory for forgetting. In J. Doris (Ed.), *The suggestibility of children's recollections* (pp. 92–105). Washington, DC: American Psychological Association.

Flin, R., Boon, J., Knox, A., & Bull, R. (1992). The effect of a five-month delay on children's and adult's eyewitness memory. *British Journal of Psychology, 83,* 323–336.

Fontes, L. A. (Ed.). (1995). Sexual abuse in nine North American cultures: Treatment and prevention. Thousand Oaks, CA: Sage.

Geiselman, R. E., Saywitz, K. J., & Bornstein, G. K. (1993). Effects of cognitive questioning techniques on children's recall performance. In G. Goodman & B. Bottoms (Eds.), *Child victims, child witnesses: Understanding and improving testimony.* New York: Guilford Press.

Goodman, G. S., & Aman, C. (1990). Children's use of anatomically detailed dolls to recount an event. *Child Development, 61,* 1859–1871.

Goodman, G. S., & Bottoms, B. L. (Eds.). (1993). *Child victims, child witnesses: Understanding and improving testimony.* New York: Guilford Press.

Goodman, G. S., Bottoms, B. L., Schwartz-Kenney, B. M., & Rudy, L. (1991). Children's testimony for a stressful event: Improving children's reports. *Journal of Narrative and Life History, 1,* 69–99.

Goodman, G. S., Sharma, A., Thomas, S. F., & Considine, M. G. (1995). Mother knows best: Effects of relationship status and interviewer bias on children's memory. *Journal of Experimental Child Psychology, 60,* 195–228.

Gordon, B. N., Ornstein, P. A., Nida, R. E., Follmer, A., Crenshaw, M. C., & Albert, G. (1993). Does the use of dolls facilitate children's memory of visits to the doctor? *Applied Cognitive Psychology, 7,* 459–474.

Green, A. (1991). Factors contributing to false allegations of child sexual abuse in custody disputes. *Child and Youth Services, 15*(3), 177–189.

Groth, N., & Stevenson, T. (1990). *Anatomical drawings for use in the investigation and intervention of child sexual abuse.* Dunedin, FL: Forensic Mental Health Associates.

Hewitt, S. (1991). Therapeutic management of preschool cases of alleged but unsubstantiated sexual abuse. *Child Welfare, 70,* 59–67.

Hill, P. E., & Hill, S. M. (1987). Videotaping children's testimony: An empirical view. *Michigan Law Review, 85,* 809–833.

Hudson, J. A., & Fivush, R. (1987). *As time goes by: Sixth graders remember a kindergarten experience. Emory Cognition Project Report #13.* Atlanta: Emory University.

Hudson, J., & Nelson, K. (1986). Repeated encounters of a similar kind: Effects of familiarity on children's autobiographical memory. *Cognitive Development, 1,* 253–271.

Hughes, M., & Grieve, R. (1980). On asking children bizarre questions. *First Language, 1,* 149–160.

Jones, D. P., & McGraw, J. M. (1987). Reliable and fictitious accounts of sexual abuse to children. *Journal of Interpersonal Violence, 2,* 27–45.

Jones, D., & Selg, A. (1988). Child sexual abuse allegations in custody or visitation cases: A report of 20 cases. In E. B. Nicholson & J. Bulkley (Eds.), *Sexual abuse allegations in custody and visitation cases* (pp. 22–36). Washington, DC: American Bar Association.

Kail, R. (1990). *The development of memory in children* (3rd ed.). New York: W. H. Freeman & Company.

Kaplan, S., & Kaplan, S. (1981). The child's accusation on sexual abuse during a divorce and custody struggle. *Hillside Journal of Clinical Psychiatry, 3,* 81–95.

Kendall-Tackett, K. A., Williams, L. M., & Finkelhor, D. (1993). Impact of sexual abuse on children: A review and synthesis of recent empirical studies. *Psychological Bulletin, 113,* 164–180.

Labov, W. (1982). Speech actions and reaction in personal narrative. In D. Tannen (Ed.), *Analyzing discourse: Text and talk.* Washington, DC: Georgetown University Press.

Lamb, M. E., Hershkowitz, I., Sternberg, K. J., Esplin, P. W., Hovav, M., Manor, T., & Yudilevitch, L. (In press). Effects of investigative utterance types on Israeli children's responses. *International Journal of Behavioral Development.*

Lamb, M., Sternberg, K., & Esplin, P. (In press). Factors influencing the reliability and validity of statements made by young victims of sexual maltreatment. *Journal of Applied Psychology.*

Large, M. E. (1995). The interview setting. *MDIC Handbook, 1,* 13-1–13-24.

Lawson, L., & Chaffin, M. (1992). False negatives in sexual abuse discosure interview: Incidence and influence of caretaker's belief in abuse in cases of accidental abuse discovery and diagnosis of STD. *Journal of Interpersonal Violence, 7*(4), 532–542.

Leichtman, M. D., & Ceci, S. J. (1995). The effects of stereotypes and suggestions on preschoolers' reports. *Developmental Psychology, 31*(4), 568–578.

Leippe, M. R., Romanczyk, A., & Manion, A. P. (1991). Eyewitness memory for a touching experience: Accuracy differences between child and adult witnesses. *Journal of Applied Psychology, 76,* 367–379.

Lepore, S., & Sesco, B. (1994). Distorting children's reports and interpretations of events through suggestion. *Journal of Applied Psychology, 79,* 108–120.

Leventhal, J. M., Hamilton, J., Rekedal, S., Tebano-Micci, A., & Eyster, C. (1989). Anatomically correct dolls used in interviews of young children suspected of having been sexually abused. *Pediatrics, 84,* 900–906.

Lewis, M., Stanger, C., & Sullivan, M. W. (1989). Deception in three year olds. *Developmental Psychology, 25,* 439–443.

Lindsay, D. S., Gonzales, V., & Eso, K. (1995). Aware and unaware uses of memories of postevent suggestions. In M. S. Zaragoza, J. R. Graham, G. C. N. Hall, R. Hirschman, & Y. S. Beh-Porath (Eds.), *Memory and testimony in the child witness.* Thousand Oaks, CA: Sage.

Loftus, F. (1979). *Eyewitness testimony.* Cambridge, MA: Harvard University Press.

London Home Office and Department of Health. (1992). *Memorandum of good practice: On video recorded interviews with child witnesses for criminal proceedings.* London: Author.

Lyon, T. D. (1996). Assessing children's competence to take the oath: Research and recommendations. *The APSAC Advisor, 9*(1), 1, 3–7.

McCabe, A., & Peterson, C. (1991). Getting the story: A longitudinal study of parental styles in eliciting narratives and developing narrative skill. In A. McCabe & C. Peterson (Eds.), *New directions in developing narrative structure.* Hillsdale, NJ: Erlbaum.

McCloskey, M., Wible, C. G., & Cohen, N. J. (1988). Is there a special flashbulb memory mechanism? *Journal of Experimental Psychology: General, 117,* 171–181.

McGough, L. S. (1994). Memory and suggestibility. In *Child witnesses: Fragile voices in the American legal system*. New Haven: Yale University Press.

McGough, L. S., & Warren, A. R. (1994). The all-important investigative interview. *Juvenile and Family Court Journal*, 13–29.

Melton, G. B., Petrila, J., Poythress, N. G., & Slobogin, C. (1987). *Psychological evaluations for the courts: A handbook for mental health professionals and lawyers*. New York: Guilford Press.

Morgan, M. (1995). *How to interview sexual abuse victims: Including the use of anatomical dolls*. Thousand Oaks, CA: Sage.

Moston, S. (1987). The suggestibility of children in interview studies. *First Language, 7*, 67–78.

Moston, S. (1990). How children interpret and respond to questions: Situational sources of suggestibility in eyewitness interviews. *Social Behavior, 5*, 155–167.

Myers, J. E. B. (1989–1990). Allegations of child sexual abuse in custody and visitation litigation: Recommendations for improved fact finding and child protection. *Journal of Family Law, 28*, 1–41.

Ney, T. (Ed.). (1995). *True and false allegations of child sexual abuse*. New York: Russell Sage.

Perry, N. W. (1992). How children remember and why they forget. *The APSAC Advisor, 5*(3), 1–2, 13–15.

Peters, D. S. (1991). The influence of stress and arousal on the child witness. In J. Doris (Ed.), *The suggestibility of children's recollections* (pp. 60–76). Washington, DC: American Psychological Association.

Pillemer, D. B., & White, S. H. (1989). Childhood events recalled by children and adults. In H. W. Reese (Ed.), *Advances in child development and behavior*. New York: Academic Press.

Pipe, M. E., Gee, S., & Wilson, C. (1993). Cues, props, and context: Do they facilitate children's event reports? In G. S. Goodman & B. L. Bottoms (Eds.), *Child victims, child witnesses: Understanding and improving testimony*. New York: Guilford Press.

Poole, D. A., & Lindsay, D. S. (1995). Interviewing preschoolers: Effects of nonsuggestive techniques, parental coaching, and leading questions on reports of non-experienced events. *Journal of Experimental Child Psychology, 60*, 129–154.

Poole, D. A., & White, L. T. (1991). Effects of question repetition on the eyewitness testimony of children and adults. *Developmental Psychology, 27*(6), 975–986.

Poole, D. A., & White, L. T. (1993). Two years later: Effects of question repetition and retention interval on the eyewitness testimony of children and adults. *Developmental Psychology, 29*(5), 844–853.

Poole, D. A., & White, L. T. (1995). Tell me again and again: Stability and change in the repeated testimonies of children and adults. In M. S. Zaragoza, J. R. Graham, G. C. N. Hall, R. Hirschman, & Y. S. Beh-Porath (Eds.), *Memory and testimony in the child witness*. Thousand Oaks, CA: Sage.

Pratt, C. (1990). On asking adults and children bizarre questions. *First Language, 10*, 167–175.

Price, D. W., & Goodman, G. S. (1990). Visiting the wizard: Children's memory for a recurring event. *Child Development, 61*, 664–680.

Rosenthal, R. (1985). From unconscious experimenter bias to teacher expectancy effects. In J. B. Dusek (Ed.), *Teacher expectancies* (pp. 37–134). Hillsdale, NJ: Erlbaum.

Rosenthal, R., & Rubin, D. B. (1978). Interpersonal expectancy effects: The first 345 studies. *Behavioral and Brain Sciences, 3,* 377–386.

Ross, D. F., Miller, B. S., & Moran, P. B. (1987). The child in the eyes of the jury: Assessing mock jurors' perceptions of child witnesses. In S. J. Ceci, M. P. Toglia, & D. F. Ross (Eds.), *Children's eyewitness memory* (pp. 142–154). New York: Springer-Verlag.

Rudy, L., & Goodman, G. S. (1991). Effects of participation on children's reports: Implications for children's testimony. *Developmental Psychology, 27*(4), 527–538.

Salmon, K., Bidrose, S., & Pipe, M. E. (1995). Providing props to facilitate children's event reports: A comparison of toys and real items. *Journal of Experimental Child Psychology, 60,* 174–194.

Saywitz, K. S., Geiselman, R. E., & Bornstein, G. (1992). Effects of cognitive interviewing and practice of children's recall. *Journal of Applied Psychology, 77*(5), 744–756.

Saywitz, K. J., Goodman, G. S., Nicholas, E., & Moan, S. (1991). Children's memories of physical examinations involving genital touch: Implications for reports of child sexual abuse. *Journal of Consulting and Clinical Psychology, 59,* 682–691.

Saywitz, K. J., & Nathanson, R. (1993). Children's testimony and their perceptions of stress in and out of the courtroom. *Child Abuse & Neglect, 17,* 613–622.

Saywitz, K. J., & Snyder, L. (1993). Improving children's testimony with preparation. In G. Goodman & B. Bottoms (Eds.), *Child victims, child witnesses: Understanding and improving testimony.* New York: Guilford Press.

Schor, D. P., & Sivan, A. B. (1989). Interpreting children's labels for sex-related body parts of anatomically explicit dolls. *Child Abuse & Neglect, 13,* 523–531.

Sobsey, D. (1994). *Violence and abuse in the lives of people with disabilities.* Baltimore, MD: Paul H. Brookes.

Sorenson, E., Bottoms, B., & Perona, A. (1997). *Handbook on intake and forensic interviewing in the Children's Advocacy Center setting.* Washington, DC: Office of Juvenile Justice and Delinquency Prevention.

Sorenson, T., & Snow, B. (1991). How children tell: The process of disclosure in child sexual abuse. *Child Welfare, 70,* 3–15.

Special education for children with disabilities. (Spring, 1996). *The Future of Children, 6*(7).

Special Issue: Facilitated Communication. (1994). *Child Abuse & Neglect, 18*(6).

Stellar, M., & Boychuk, T. (1992). Children as witnesses in sexual abuse cases: Investigative interview and assessment techniques. In H. Dent & R. Flin (Eds.), *Children as witnesses.* Chichester, England: Wiley.

Stern, P. (1997). *Preparing and presenting expert testimony in child abuse litigation: A guide for expert witnesses and attorneys.* Thousand Oaks, CA: Sage.

Steward, M. (1989, November). *The development of a model interview for young child victims of sexual abuse* (final report to the National Center on Child Abuse and Neglect). Davis: University of California, Davis, Department of Psychiatry.

234 A CHILD INTERVIEWER'S GUIDEBOOK

Steward, M. S., Bussey, K., Goodman, G. S., & Saywitz, K. J. (1993). Implications of developmental research for interviewing children. *Child Abuse & Neglect, 17,* 25–37.

Stouthamer-Loeber, M. (1987, April). *Mothers' perceptions of children's lying and its relationship to behavior problems.* Presented at the meeting of the Society for Research on Child Development, Baltimore, MD.

Summit, R. C. (1983). The child sexual abuse accommodation syndrome. *Child Abuse & Neglect, 7,* 177–193.

Tate, C. S., & Warren-Leubecker, A. (1989, April). The effects of adult coaching on children's willingness to provide false reports. Presented at the meeting of the Society for Research on Child Development, Kansas City, MO.

Tate, C., Warren, A., & Hess, T. (1992). Adults' liability for children's "lie-ability": Can adults coach children to lie successfully? In S. J. Ceci, M. D. Leichtman, & M. E. Putnick (Eds.), *Cognitive and social factors in early deception* (pp. 69–87). New York: Macmillan.

Terr, L. (1988). What happens to early memories of trauma? A study of twenty children under age five at the time of documented traumatic events. *Journal of the American Academy of Child and Adolescent Psychiatry, 27,* 96–104.

Tharinger, D., Burrows-Horton, C., & Millea, S. (1990). Sexual abuse and exploitation of children and adults with mental retardation and other handicaps. *Child Abuse & Neglect, 14,* 301–312.

Thoennes, N., & Tjaden, P. G. (1990). The extent, nature and validity of sexual abuse allegations in custody/visitation dispute. *Child Abuse & Neglect, 14,* 151–163.

Tobey, A., & Goodman, G. S. (1992). Children's eyewitness memory: Effects of participation and forensic context. *Child Abuse & Neglect, 16,* 779–796.

Toglia, M. P., Ross, D. F., Ceci, S. J., & Hembrooke, H. (1992). The suggestibility of children's memory: A social-psychological and cognitive interpretation. In M. L. Howe, C. J. Brainer, & V. F. Reyna (Eds.), *Development of long-term retention.* New York: Springer-Verlag.

Valenti-Hein, D., & Schwartz, L. (1995). The maltreatment of intellectually handicapped children and adolescents. *Child Abuse & Neglect, 19,* 205–215.

van de Kamp, J. K. (1986). *Report on the Kern County Child Abuse Investigation.* Office of the Attorney General, Division of Law Enforcement Bureau of Investigation, Kern County, California.

van der Kolk, B. (1994). The body keeps the score: Memory and the evolving psychobiology of posttraumatic stress. *Harvard Review of Psychiatry, 1,* 253–265.

Verdugo, M., Bermeho, B., & Fuertes, J. (1995). The maltreatment of intellectually handicapped children and adolescents. *Child Abuse & Neglect, 19,* 105–215.

Walker, A. G. (1994). *Handbook on questioning children: A linguistic perspective.* Washington, DC: American Bar Association Center on Children and the Law.

Walker, A. G. (1997, January). *Understanding children's language.* Paper presented at the San Diego Conference on Responding to Child Maltreatment, San Diego, CA.

Warren, A. R., Hulse-Trotter, K., & Tubbs, E. (1991). Inducing resistance to suggestibility in children. *Law and Human Behavior, 15,* 273–285.

Warren, A. R., & Lane, P. (1995). Effects of timing and type of questioning on eyewitness accuracy and suggestibility. In M. S. Zaragoza, J. R. Graham, G. C. N. Hall, R. Hirschman, & Y. S. Ben-Porath (Eds.), *Memory and testimony in the child witness* (pp. 44–60). Thousand Oaks, CA: Sage.

Warren, A. R., Woodall, C. E., Hunt, J. S., & Perry, N. W. (1996). "It sounds good in theory, but . . .": Do investigative interviewers follow guidelines based on memory research? *Child Maltreatment, 1*(3), 231–245.

Wilson, J. C., & Pipe, M. E. (1989). The effects of cues on young children's recall of real events. *New Zealand Journal of Psychology, 18*, 65–70.

Yuille, J. C., Hunter, R., Joffe, R., & Zaparniuk, J. (1993). Interviewing children in sexual abuse cases. In G. S. Goodman & B. L. Bottoms (Eds.), *Child victims, child witnesses: Understanding and improving testimony.* New York: Guilford Press.

Index

About the Authors

Wendy Bourg, PhD, has worked as a Child Interviewer at the C. A. R. E. S. (Child Abuse Response and Evaluation Services) Northwest Program for the past 5 years. In that capacity, she has evaluated close to 1,000 children. Currently, she is establishing a Research Center at C. A. R. E. S. Northwest. She has written articles and book chapters on topics such as children of divorce and domestic violence, and the development of adult anxiety disorders. She has provided numerous trainings on child interviewing in the Portland, Oregon, area and throughout the state of Oregon.

Raymond Broderick, BA, is Director of the Lane County, Oregon, Child Advocacy Center. Since 1976, he has been an investigator with the Lane County District Attorney's office. He is the only sworn law enforcement officer in the United States to head a child advocacy center. He designed state-of-the-art video interview rooms at his center, and, since 1995, has video-interviewed over 1,000 children. He provides local, regional, and national training and consultation in the areas of communication and deception within interviews, and is a member of the APSAC's sub-committee on videotaping. As a national proponent of videotaping child interviews, he promotes video interviews as the best way to present, as evidence, nonverbal and verbal communication between child and interviewer.

Robin Flagor, BSW, is a child interviewer with Merle West Medical Center's Klamath-Lake C. A. R. E. S. Program. Previously, she worked for approximately 9 years as a front line emergency response child protective services worker in two states. Her professional interest has always included working with child abuse victims. She has worked in a variety of settings and in different capacities with abused children, including as a runaway crisis line worker, runaway shelter counselor, group home counselor, group home social worker, child and family therapist within a school district, family reunification caseworker, and Child Protective Services intake worker.

Donna Meeks Kelly, JD, has been an attorney in Oregon since 1982. She has been in private practice both as an associate of a firm and as a sole practitioner. Since January 1995, she has served as a Deputy District Attorney prosecuting child abuse cases on a full-time basis for Hood River, Wasco, and Sherman Counties. She is well-known as a strong advocate for children and has been a leader on a number of boards and agencies serving children, including the Juvenile Services Commission in Hood River County. In 1997 she was appointed to the Children's Trust Fund of Oregon by Oregon Governor John Kitzhaber.

Diane Lang Ervin, MSW, LCSW, is a licensed clinical social worker at St. Charles Medical Center in Bend, Oregon, and has worked in the field of medical social work since 1980. Her most recent experience includes 2 years as a Child Interviewer at KIDS Center in Bend, Oregon, conducting videotaped interviews with children who are alleged to have been sexually abused. She has testified as an expert witness in various court settings and has designed and developed staff training courses and provided educational inservices in child abuse and neglect and other related areas throughout central Oregon.

Judy Butler, MEd, is Clinical Supervisor of the Interviewers at C. A. R. E. S. Northwest, a medically based child abuse assessment center in Portland, Oregon. She has been working in the field of child welfare since 1970. Her primary focus since the late 1970s has been the evaluation and treatment of children who are alleged to have been sexually abused. She assisted in data collection for research projects on child sexual behavior under the direction of Dr. William Friedrich of the Mayo Clinic, and has provided extensive training and consultation throughout Oregon. With Pamela Crow, she co-authored *Helping Children Recover From Sexual Abuse: A Guide for Parents.*

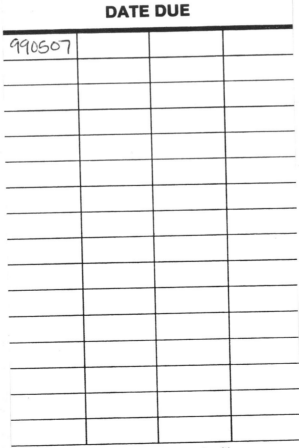

DATE DUE

990507			

#47-0108 Peel Off Pressure Sensitive